ELTbasics

A Beginner's Guide to ENGLISH LANGUAGE TEACHING

JAN EDWARDS DORMER

This book has a companion website.
Go to www.tesol.org/ELTBasics for additional resources.

www.tesol.org/bookstore

TESOL International Association
1925 Ballenger Avenue, Ste. 550
Alexandria, VA 22314 USA
www.tesol.org

Managing Editor: Tomiko Breland
Head of Education & Events: Sarah Sahr
Copy Editor: Tomiko Breland
Manuscript Reviewers: Keith Graham, Khanh-Duc Kuttig, Rachel Lamb, Irina Levy
Cover Design: Elisabeth Heissler Design
Interior Design and Layout: Citrine Sky Design

Copyright © 2023 by TESOL International Association

All rights reserved. Copying or further publication of the contents of this work is not permitted without permission of TESOL International Association, except for limited "fair use" for educational, scholarly, and similar purposes as authorized by U.S. Copyright Law, in which case appropriate notice of the source of the work should be given. Permission to reproduce material from this book must be obtained from www.copyright.com, or contact Copyright Clearance Center, Inc., 222 Rosewood Drive, Danvers, MA 01923, 978-750-8400

Every effort has been made to copyright holders for permission to reprint borrowed material. We regret any oversights that may have occurred and will rectify them in future printings of this work.

The publications of the TESOL Press present a variety of viewpoints. The views expressed or implied in this publication, unless otherwise noted, should not be interpreted as official positions of the organization.

Recommended citation:
Dormer, J. E. (2023). *ELT Basics: A beginner's guide to English language teaching*. TESOL International Association.

ISBN 978-1-953745-16-3
ISBN (ebook) 978-1-953745-17-0
Library of Congress Control Number 2023931596

Table of Contents

Introduction vii

Chapter 1. Understanding Language 1

Chapter 2. Understanding Language Acquisition 10

Chapter 3. Addressing Difference: Considering Individual Contexts,
Students, and Teachers 28

Chapter 4. Planning and Teaching English Language Lessons 42

Chapter 5. Assessment in ELT 69

Chapter 6. ELT Skills and Activities 86

Chapter 7. Charting a Course for ELT Development 125

Glossary 132

References 135

Appendixes
    A. Acronyms in ELT 137
    B. Sample Worksheets 139
    C. Resources 143

This book is dedicated to my students around the world.

Asante sana. Terima kasih. Muchas gracias. Merci. Obrigada.
اشكرك. ありがとうございます. 감사합니다. 谢谢你.

Thank you for your willingness to invest in English language learning and teaching, and in our learning communities. Thank you for your friendship and trust. May you continue to grow and impact others through this wonderfully diverse and rich field of English language teaching.

Introduction

English language teaching (ELT) is teaching English to people who are learning English as a new language. These learners already speak one or more other languages; they are learning English as an additional language.

There are many different contexts in which the English language is taught. Following are some of these contexts:

- Foreign language classrooms in countries where English is not a dominant language
- English language schools where students study only English (These schools might have programs for different age groups. They also might have specialized courses, such as test preparation courses or courses for specific professions, such as business.)
- Bilingual or dual language programs, where English is used as one of the mediums of instruction
- Schools that are fully in English, where students are receiving some English language instruction, but are also hearing and using English in all their classes
- English-learning programs for adults who might be immigrants or refugees
- University programs for international students
- Workplace programs catering to the language needs of a specific workplace

These are only some of the possible contexts where English is being taught as an additional language. Any place where students are learning English and where there is active instruction to help them is an ELT context.

Terms

There are also many different terms used for learning and teaching English. You can find a resource for understanding many of these terms in Appendix A. Here are just a few of the most common terms that you might have seen or heard:

Context-Related Terms

- **EFL** (English as a foreign language): This term is sometimes used to talk about learning English within a society where English *is not* the dominant language.
- **ESL** (English as a second language): This term is sometimes used to talk about learning English within a society where English *is* the dominant language.
- **ESOL** (English for speakers of other languages): This term refers to learning English in any context when English is not the first language.
- **TESOL** (teachers of English to speakers of other languages): This term is sometimes used for the field or profession of ELT.

Learner-Related Terms

- **ELL or EL:** English language learner or English learner: This term is sometimes used to describe someone who is learning English as a new language.
- **MLL** (multilingual learner): This term is sometimes used for language learners in recognition of the student's other rich language skills.
- **MLE** (multilingual learner of English): This term is sometimes used for learners of English, specifically, also in recognition of the student's other rich language skills.

In the past, sometimes terms were used for learners that emphasized a language deficit, or that reflected a deficit-based way of thinking about language learners. For example, English learners in the United States were sometimes called "limited English proficient" and referred to as LEP students. It's important to recognize all the language skills that students have, in home languages and languages being acquired, and to use terms that value students' diverse language skills. There has been a movement in the ELT field toward asset-based terms and ways of looking at learners, such as using the term "multilingual learner of English" (MLE), which draws attention to students' existing language skills and does not frame lack of language knowledge as a deficit.

In this book, the term *ELT* is used to describe English language teaching in any context. A person who is learning English is referred to in different ways, depending on the context. Terms used might include *student, English learner, multilingual learner of English*, or others that are relevant to the topic of discussion.

Training for ELT

Ideally, all teachers of the English language have training in language teaching. Training programs for teaching the English language include those offered in university teacher preparation programs and shorter "certificate" level training. However, sometimes teachers begin teaching the English language before they have had the opportunity to receive training. This book aims to meet the needs of these teachers, while also serving as a review, quick guide, or resource for those who have basic, limited, or partial training.

Overview of This Book

This book begins in Chapters 1 and 2 with important background knowledge in understanding language and language acquisition. The remainder of the book focuses on the practice of ELT.

Chapter 3 highlights the many differences in learners and contexts in the field of ELT. English is learned around the world by students of all ages, in many different kinds of schools and programs, for many different purposes. This chapter addresses these differences and how they impact ELT.

Chapter 4 gets to the heart of ELT, addressing the planning and teaching of English language lessons. Sample lesson plans are provided, and teaching skills, such as providing feedback, are addressed.

Chapter 5 addresses the assessment of language learning and various uses of assessment. Important concepts, such as tailoring assessment systems to learners' goals, aligning assessment with instruction, and considering cultural impacts on assessment, are covered.

Chapter 6 describes numerous activities that can be used in English language lessons. Activities are sorted into the categories of "speaking and listening," "reading and writing," and "integrated skills." Each activity includes information about the types of students and teaching points for which it could be effective.

Chapter 7 outlines different types of training programs for becoming an ELT professional. This chapter includes information about the different content and purposes of short-term training programs versus longer university-level programs, with guidance provided for evaluating training programs.

All the terms in bold throughout the book are found in the glossary on page 132. Readers can use this resource to quickly recall the meaning of a term in the field of ELT.

Finally, the appendixes provide useful resources, including a guide to acronyms, some sample worksheets, and ELT web resources.

CHAPTER 1

Understanding Language

Language is complex and multifaceted. This chapter discusses the different ways that people view language, and the reality that language is fluid and dynamic because it occurs within communities of language users. We will discuss the four **language domains** and the three dimensions of language: **form**, **meaning**, and **use**. Finally, this chapter addresses the differences between social and academic or professional language, and the impact of culture on language.

Language as a System; Language as Communication

There are different ideas about what it means to study, know, or learn a language. In all perspectives, people recognize the importance of knowing words. The words of a language are the starting point of knowing a language. But what is done with those words may be different depending on whether someone sees language more as a system or more as a means of communication. Sometimes, language classes focus on learning grammar rules. In these classes, students are learning *about* the language (as a system), but they are not using it for real communication (acquiring the ability to communicate in the language). Native speakers have learned the language primarily for real communication. They use the language well but may know very little about the systems of the language. Language is both a system and communication. One way to understand how these go together is this: Language is a system that is used for communication.

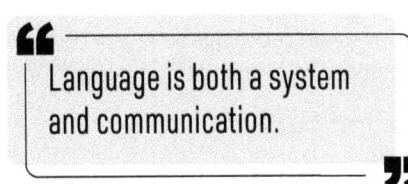

Language is both a system and communication.

Language as a system includes grammar, sometimes called **structures**; written symbols (such as the English alphabet); and the sounds of language, or its **phonology**. Language as a system tells us that the sentence "She black hair has" is not possible in English. It also tells us that *pan* and *pen*, though very similar, have different vowel sounds in English, and are two different words.

Language is also communication. The incorrect sentence "She black hair has" probably will still result in communication. Most English speakers can understand what the speaker is trying to communicate. However, the perfectly correct sentence "Could you please close the door?" could be misunderstood. The structure is a question, but the speaker isn't really asking for an answer. This is a request, and the response should be to close the door.

Effective English language teaching (ELT) requires an understanding of language as both a system and as communication—of language as a system used to communicate. Sometimes, language classes don't achieve this balance. For example, a language class might provide grammar lessons, but students might not be using the grammar they are learning for communication. In another example, students might be talking a lot with each other, but the teacher might not be providing feedback to help them communicate more accurately.

English learners should view language as a means of expressing ideas. A large part of what occurs in ELT should involve real communication in oral and written forms. This is often called "communicative language teaching." (You will learn more about this and other methodologies in Chapters 2, 3, and 4.) However, the system of language provides the building blocks for achieving this communication. Without a shared system of grammar, sounds, and symbols, ideas cannot be communicated.

"Correct" Language

Language communities develop as groups of people use language to communicate with each other for specific purposes. Because English is used in very different places and ways around the world, there are many different English-using communities. What may be considered "correct" English in one may be considered incorrect in another. The following concepts contribute to these perceptions of what language is "right":

- nativeness
- correctness
- translanguaging

Let's discuss these further.

Nativeness

Many people think that "native speaker" English is best and that native speaker–like proficiency is the standard that English learners should aspire to. Sometimes, being a native speaker of English is listed as a requirement for English teaching jobs. This perspective discriminates against highly proficient, well-trained English language teachers who simply may not have learned English as their first language. In addition, the term "native speaker-like" is sometimes used to describe someone who speaks an additional language very well, instead of simply saying that the person has high proficiency. All of these uses of the label "native speaker" are problematic. Let's look at why.

To begin with, determining who is a native speaker is harder than it might seem. Consider the examples in Table 1:

TABLE 1. Problems With the Term "Native Speaker": Examples

Speaker	Native Language
Maria grows up speaking Spanish and English, but only speaking Spanish at a high proficiency level.	Is Maria a native speaker of both languages?
Amari only speaks Arabic until he goes to school. But because all his schooling is in English, he becomes more proficient in English than in Arabic.	Which language is ultimately Amari's native language?
Chiyo grew up speaking Japanese, and then learned English as an adult. Now, she uses English professionally and has more professional and academic proficiency in English.	Has English become Chiyo's native language?

These situations reveal problems with using "native speaker" as a standard, requirement, or descriptor.

Even if it were easy to determine who is a native speaker, the goal of sounding like a native speaker is not a very useful one. English has many **dialects**. A dialect is a specific form of a language, usually spoken within a region, or spoken by a particular group of people. On one hand, two "native speakers" of English might use English very differently, because they speak different dialects. On the other hand, a native speaker and a nonnative speaker of the same dialect might have very similar speech and language usage. It's much more helpful to talk about levels of proficiency (which are addressed in Chapter 5). For example, terms such as "fluent English speaker" or "fully proficient English user" can be used instead of "native speaker" to indicate full English proficiency.

TESOL International Association, the largest professional organization for teachers of the English language, has spoken out against the practice of only hiring "native English speakers" for English teaching positions. (TESOL's position statement on this practice can be found on the companion website for this book.) We can all help to promote the perspective that teaching skill and English language proficiency are needed for effective language teaching, not "nativeness."

Correctness

ELT fundamentally involves helping multilingual learners of English produce language that is correct and effective in achieving its intended communication purposes. Knowing what language is "correct" can be challenging. Different language communities use language in different ways, and what may be acceptable in one community might not be in another. For example, the sentence "He walk everyday" lacks the "–s" on "walk" that is necessary in third-person singular present tense in standard English dialects. However, this sentence is acceptable in some colloquial dialects. It's impossible to say whether this sentence is correct or incorrect without specifying the dialect and language community.

There are two perspectives on language correctness:

- ➤ *Prescriptive:* There are language rules that must be followed, even if the language changes and people stop following those rules.
- ➤ *Descriptive:* Languages evolve and change based on how communities use them.

This book adheres to the descriptive perspective when it comes to teaching language. Have you ever heard someone say, "I know it's wrong, but everybody says it that way"? This statement contradicts what we know about languages. If "everyone" in a given community says something in the same way, then it can be seen as correct within that dialect (descriptive). The prescriptive perspective runs counter to the reality that languages change as language communities change how they use language.

Translanguaging

A final concept to understand about what language is "right" to use is that of **translanguaging**: When students utilize their full linguistic repertoire, including linguistic features of multiple languages, to maximize communication. The term "**code-switching**" is a related, and perhaps better known term, which refers to switching between languages during communication, and which sometimes has a negative connotation. Some institutions frown upon the use of the home language within the English language classroom. These schools and programs sometimes have "English only" policies forbidding the use of all languages in the classroom except English, arguing that if students are allowed to rely on another language, they won't learn English.

The word *translanguaging* emerged to describe the beneficial and effective use of more than one language for purposes such as communicating within multilingual groups and nurturing cultural identities. When learning a new language, it is important not to lose other languages. Rather, the home language and other languages the student speaks should be valued, maintained, and further developed, if possible. Translanguaging can be a useful tool in realizing this goal.

The goal of ELT is to help students develop the type of English they need or want in order to communicate within the type of context they envision for themselves. Obviously, when students are communicating in English with those who don't speak their home language, they likely need to be equipped for communication solely in English. This goal, however, does not negate the fact that there are useful roles for students' home and other languages as they are learning English.

Language Domains

There are four primary domains of language:

1. Listening
2. Speaking
3. Reading
4. Writing

These are sometimes called the skills of language.

- Listening and reading are **receptive skills**: ways in which we receive language.
- Speaking and writing are **productive skills**: ways in which we produce language in order to communicate.

We can also categorize these domains as oral (listening and speaking) and written (reading and writing). Though it's common to hear language knowledge framed as "speaking the language," often people really mean that a person can use all four of these domains.

There are ELT contexts in which the goal is not necessarily to achieve high proficiency in all four domains. For example, a person visiting a country for a short time might only need oral proficiency in basic topics. However, a person residing in a country where English isn't used may just want strong reading and writing skills for global engagement through the internet. The teaching of English should involve assessing students' needs for English and their goals in learning it, and efforts to tailor the learning program to those needs. More information on assessment is provided in Chapter 5.

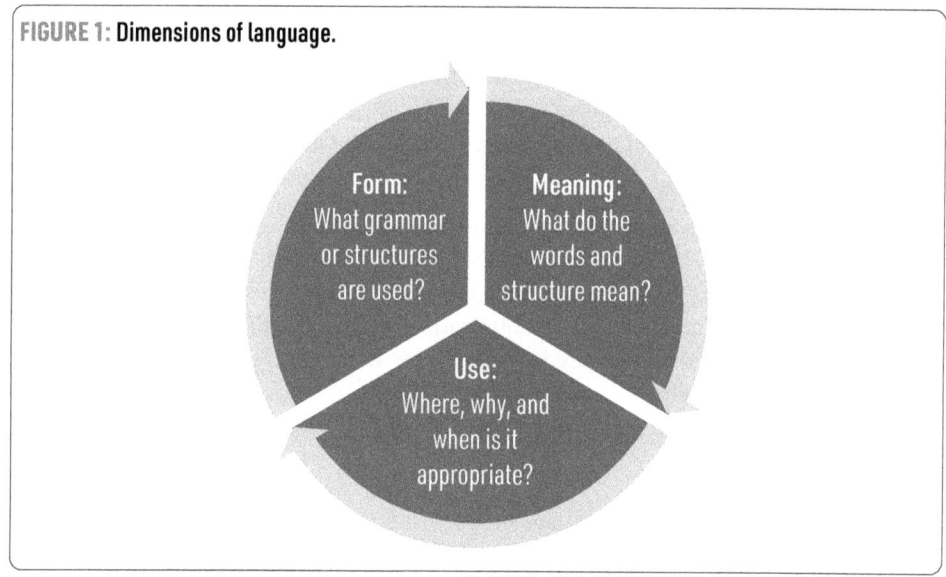

FIGURE 1: Dimensions of language.

Form, Meaning, and Use

Language can also be viewed through the dimensions of form, meaning, and use (see Figure 1).

Form

The *form* of language is the structure it takes: its grammatical features. The English sentence "I have book" has an error in form. In standard varieties of English, the article "a" is needed, or "book" should be changed to the plural "books."

Meaning

Language also has *meaning*: It is conveying an idea to the listener or reader. Language forms are fairly straightforward, but language meaning may not be. Idiomatic language, inferences, and implications all have meanings that are not directly stated. For example, if a teacher says "Would you please take out your workbooks?" the form is a question, but the sentence is actually a command: The students must take out their workbooks.

Use

Finally, language is *used* in particular ways: In any given language community, a member of that community knows rules governing language use. To illustrate this, consider the sentence "I have 29 years." To English speakers, this is the wrong way to state your age in English. Why is it wrong? The form of the sentence is not wrong. There is no overt grammar error. The meaning is fairly clear: Most people will understand that age is the topic of the sentence. But there is still an error. It's an error in use. Though "I have 29 years" is the way age is stated in many languages, in English, the correct usage is "I am 29."

Social and Academic or Professional English

A distinction that is relevant in many ELT contexts is the difference between social and academic or professional language. Social language may be achieved relatively quickly. A person might become highly proficient communicating in social contexts within 1–2 years, but academic or professional competence in a language might take 5–7 years.

Academic or professional language competence includes knowing specialized words, such as the word *theorem* in geometry or the word *stethoscope* in medical professions. It also includes words and phrases that simply are not common in informal oral language use, such as *therefore* and *in other words*. Academic or professional language also uses more complex sentence constructions. Take this sentence, for example: "Despite having many failures as he attempted to create an electric light bulb, Thomas Edison's persistence paid off, and he eventually succeeded." There are four distinct clauses in this sentence, and readers must be able to interpret how each relates to the others. This type of language is generally not found in social usage and takes much longer to acquire.

Language and Culture

Knowing a language is only one part of language proficiency. Language is used within cultures, and these cultures often play a role in communication. ELT contexts differ greatly in what aspects of culture are relevant. For example, an immigrant child learning English in an Australian school will have a very high need to learn Australian school culture alongside the English language, whereas Japanese and Malaysian business partners communicating in English may not need to know very much about the cultural norms governing English usage in English-majority countries. In another example, a multilingual learner of English in the United States who experiences an awkward silence after asking an older woman her age or asking a neighbor how much he paid for his new car will quickly learn that language competence isn't only about knowing the right words and grammar: It's also about when, where, and with whom to use them.

When it comes to speaking English in a country where English is the dominant language, learning about the culture and cultural cues can be essential to successful interactions. Most people are not aware of how much culture influences the words we say, how we say them, and how we interpret the words of others. Think for a moment about greetings. A person usually learns greetings early in the language acquisition process. But a person must also learn what expressions are used with whom, and under what circumstances. For example, are different greetings appropriate at a sports event and at a formal dinner? Does the age of the person matter? Does social status in relation to that person matter? How quickly are greetings concluded and the move made to the topic of conversation? In some cultures, this transition happens much more slowly than in others, and launching too quickly into the topic can be seen as rude and insensitive. To communicate effectively, one must learn not only the language, but also the culture within which it is used.

Snow (2007) discusses culture as being composed of shared knowledge, shared views, and shared patterns. For example, a piece of shared knowledge in American culture is that the Thanksgiving holiday is spent with family. A shared view is that creativity and individualism are valued and encouraged. A shared pattern is that meetings are marked with set start times, and people are present and ready to begin at that time.

When applied specifically to the use of the English language within a culture, shared knowledge might include the fact that "I'm good" is an affirmative response to a greeting, not a claim of personal virtue. English speakers might share the view that productivity is more important in the workplace than relationship building, and therefore hallway conversations should be limited to very short exchanges. A shared pattern might be that it's fine to spend little or no time on small talk at the beginning of a conversation, getting quickly to the topic at hand.

These examples merely scratch the surface of the many ways in which culture affects language.

Chapter Summary

This chapter has talked about what language is, and how people use language for different purposes in different contexts. Here are some key points in this chapter:

> Understanding language is the necessary starting point for understanding ELT.
> It's important to value the goal of communicating in English while understanding that some learning about the systems of English can facilitate reaching this goal.
> Language occurs within communities, which may use the same language in different ways.
> While a student's goal may be to learn a standard variety of English, other dialects of English and other languages should be valued and supported.
> The domains of language are listening, speaking, reading, and writing, and language includes the dimensions of form, meaning, and use.
> Language can be learned for social purposes or for academic or professional purposes.
> Often, learning English requires navigating cultural connections and students' cultures, as well as acquiring cross-cultural understanding related to students' goals for learning and using English.

The many facets of language highlight the need to identify student goals and needs in learning English, and translate those into meaningful classroom learning.

CHAPTER 2

Understanding Language Acquisition

How do people learn languages? Do we learn additional languages in the same way that we learn our first language? What is the role of instruction in learning a new language? This chapter addresses these questions, beginning with understanding how people learn their first language, often called their native language or mother tongue. Sometimes, we refer to this as the "home language" or the **L1** (the first language).

The remainder of the chapter provides information about learning an additional, new, second, or foreign language—sometimes called the **L2** (the second language; additional languages can be referred to L3, L4, and so on—usually, the numbers indicate the order in which the languages were learned). This term can be misleading, though, because many people know more than two languages, and it's unwise to assume a language being learned is the learner's second. (This is one reason "English as an additional language" is a more encompassing term than "English as a second language" when discussing groups of students.)

The language being learned can also be referred to as the **target language**. This chapter addresses theories and misconceptions of **second language acquisition** (SLA) and ends with eight key concepts about language acquisition that are important in English language teaching (ELT).

Theories

First Language Acquisition

People begin acquiring their native language even before birth, and different theories have been proposed for how this acquisition occurs. Skinner (1957) explained first language acquisition as imitation and reinforcement, also known as behaviorism. For example, a child would hear "Daddy," say "da-da," then receive positive feedback, prompting him to say "da-da" again and again. Clearly, imitation accounts for a lot of our initial language learning. Children do hear language and do imitate what they hear. However, behaviorism cannot account for the creativity that humans bring to language use. Children produce many utterances that they have not heard anyone say. These would include sentences with errors, such as "me want cookie," and novel sentences, such as "the trees are blue," perhaps in reference to the child's creative color choices when coloring a picture. A child would not have heard these utterances, so they do not produce them as a result of imitation.

Chomsky (1959) challenged Skinner's assertions with his development of universal grammar. Chomsky argued for an innatist position, that human beings are programmed to develop language. This was the only explanation, he claimed, for the fact that people can create grammatically correct utterances that they have never heard before. A related concept is the critical period hypothesis (Lenneberg, 1967). This is the idea that there is a "critical age" beyond which the first language cannot be easily acquired. Often, this critical age is said to coincide with puberty.

In the 1990s, psychology became more central to language learning research, prompting theories in which cognition plays a key role. Critics of Chomsky argued that the universal grammar explanation was not necessary because all language learning could be accounted for by more general learning theories. In other words, how we learn language is how we learn anything. A key concept that stems from this perspective is cognitive constructivism: the view that people mentally construct meanings that make sense to them, and this is how they learn (Piaget, 1951). First language acquisition would be explained, then, by the simple fact that language use is part of living our lives and meeting our needs, and that the task of survival results in language acquisition.

Some researchers have focused more on the social conditions that promote language learning than on what actually happens in the brain. Vygotsky (1978) proposed that learning takes place when an individual interacts with an interlocutor who is a more knowledgeable peer or teacher within a **zone of proximal development** (ZPD), which is the cognitive space just beyond the learner's current understanding. Vygotsky's work has often been linked to social constructivism. Whereas cognitive constructivism focuses on the mental construction of understanding, social constructivism focuses on the collaborative construction of meaning, through social interaction. Vygotsky's theory of ZPD was not limited to language acquisition. It attempted to explain development and learning in general.

However, many studies have shown that children do learn their first language through interaction. In one study, infants displayed a much greater awareness of sound differences in a foreign language introduced at 9 months when language was spoken by a loving caregiver than when it was presented through video. And even if infants are exposed to a multitude of nonlanguage sounds, it is the language sounds coming from a human in close proximity that they will attempt to imitate (Kuhl, 2010).

Additional/Second Language Acquisition

By the time a child begins attending school, they have learned their first language well. By this age, they will have acquired the basic structure and word sets of their first language. They will continue to learn more, of course, when they start reading and writing and learning academic language. If this person is exposed to a new language any time after they begin formal schooling, it is usually called an *additional* language. As mentioned earlier, this new language is often called a second language, and the field that studies the acquisition of additional languages is often referred to as second language acquisition (SLA).

Stages of second language acquisition

As learners go through the process of acquiring all the elements of a second language, they will go through stages. The following six stages, based on five stages originally outlined by Krashen and Terrell (1983), may describe the progress of a learner who is developing all four primary skills (reading, writing, speaking, and listening) as they acquire a new language.

- **Preproduction:** Learners hear or read the new language and begin to acquire it receptively. Though learners may feel comfortable repeating words and simple phrases, they are not yet able to put words together in sentences. This stage is sometimes called "the silent period." Some learners may feel more comfortable with written than spoken language at this stage.

- **Early production:** Learners acquire basic word sets and sentence structures. They begin to produce simple sentences, but continue to acquire language primarily through reception.

- **Speech emergence:** Learners begin to form longer sentences, still relying heavily on context cues and familiar topics. Language begins to increase in complexity, but errors are frequent.

- **Beginning fluency:** Language users produce basic social language fairly easily and fluently and can often write on familiar topics. They still struggle with more complex language in unfamiliar contexts. Vocabulary gaps impede communication on unfamiliar topics.

- **Intermediate fluency:** Language users can communicate fluently on a range of topics. They can use language through all modalities (reading, writing, speaking, listening) to further their learning. Errors are not frequent and do not impede communication.

- **Advanced fluency:** Language users can engage successfully in most tasks requiring language, both in social settings and in academic or professional settings. They can fully express themselves through writing, both socially and academically or professionally.

All students acquiring English as an additional language go through stages similar to these.

The phrase *language learning* is more familiar to many than *language acquisition*. These terms often mean the same thing. In some theories, however, language learning and language acquisition are two different processes. Acquisition takes place through exposure to and usage of the language, and is sometimes linked to the ability to communicate in the language. Learning, though, may refer to knowing *about* a language—having information about its grammar, vocabulary, and pronunciation—but perhaps not being able to use it for communicative purposes.

Some of the theories about first language acquisition have also been applied to SLA. Belief in behaviorism as a way that people learned new languages led to the development of the audiolingual method, or audiolingualism (Richards & Rodgers, 2001). This approach focused heavily on drills and repetition. Through audiolingualism, drilling, repetition, and memorization became equated with language learning. Though behaviorism has taken a lesser role as newer theories of language learning have emerged, it does provide a good explanation for the development of **automaticity** in language learning—the ability to use language chunks automatically and without much thought. Without automaticity, we would have to think of every word and structure before we spoke, and the cognitive load would make it very difficult to communicate.

Chomsky's (1959) innatist perspective was also applied to SLA. One influential theorist within this perspective is Krashen (1977, 1981) and his monitor model. He described this model in terms of five hypotheses:

1. **The acquisition–learning hypothesis:** We *acquire* language through exposure, but we *learn* language through study.

2. **The monitor hypothesis:** The *acquired* system initiates utterances, but the *learned* system monitors and edits them.

3. **The natural order hypothesis:** Language features are acquired in a predictable sequence, which is roughly the same for all language learners. (This concept has also been called the internal syllabus.)

4. **The input hypothesis:** Acquisition occurs when the learner is exposed to language that is comprehensible but a bit above the learner's current operational level. In other words, the learner needs to receive **comprehensible input**. Krashen framed this as "i + 1", where *i* represents the learner's current level and stands for *interlanguage* (but which we can refer to as the *independent* level) and *+1* represents a step above that level.

5. **The affective filter hypothesis:** A person's general emotional state affects language learning, either facilitating or hindering it.

Krashen's notion of i+1 is much like Vygotsky's ZPD. However, the ZPD focuses on the interaction, while i+1 refers to the level of language input, whether or not through interaction.

This theory and others helped to move language learning from rules and drills to communicative methodologies (often known as **communicative language teaching**, or CLT). Still widely followed today, communicative methods focus on learning language through real communication, rather than through isolated rules and drills.

Another key perspective in SLA is this importance of interaction. The interaction hypothesis (Long, 1981) suggests that it is communication with others that triggers language acquisition. For example, input could be achieved by listening to a recording of a dialogue taking place in a market between a buyer and a seller, but acquisition may only take place if the learner is a participant in such a dialogue. Swain (1985) extended the input hypothesis by creating an output hypothesis. She argues that it's only as students attempt to formulate comprehensible output that they notice and revise their own language use. Another insight from cognitive research is the importance of noticing or awareness. For example, a student may not internalize the *-ed* verb ending as the way we talk about the past until they begin to notice the *-ed* endings on verbs.

Finally, just as social interaction was found to affect first language acquisition, it also plays a role in acquiring an additional language. Vygotsky's ZPD has become influential in the field of SLA. We know that interaction with others in the new language is a key means by which the new language is acquired.

The theories and research presented in this section are not mutually exclusive. In fact, they all explain different parts of the language acquisition puzzle. Behaviorism may explain the learning of words and language chunks that are heard frequently. Cognition no doubt plays a role when a language learner stops to think about which verb tense to use, or where an adjective belongs in relation to a noun. And the fact that language is learned by using it socially, in communication with others, would rarely be questioned. In short, each of these theories has built on the others, and likely all have relevance in any comprehensive explanation of additional language acquisition.

Misconceptions

Most people have not learned about SLA theories. However, because everyone speaks at least one language and many people learn additional languages, opinions about language acquisition are commonplace. There are many popular notions about how people learn languages. Some of these, though widely believed, are not supported by research. This section looks at these incorrect beliefs around learning an additional language.

Misconception #1: Children Learn Languages More Easily and Quickly Than Adults

Children often do seem to "pick up" languages in ways that adults may not. Young children do have an advantage where pronunciation is concerned. They can often more easily hear and copy foreign sounds, perhaps with little effort. Because pronunciation is one of the first characteristics of language use that is noticed, good pronunciation can result in the perception that language skills are higher than they actually are. However, pronunciation is only one aspect of language. Teens and adults often have other advantages in SLA, such as greater ability to learn new words and grammar structures, better focus and retention, and stronger motivation.

Many studies have disproved a simple correlation between young age and facility in language acquisition. For example, Snow and Hoefnagel-Hohle (1982) conducted research with native English speakers of all ages who were learning Dutch as a second language. In their study, children 3–5 years old scored the lowest on language tests, in all categories. Older children, teens, and adults all outperformed the youngest group of children. Sometimes, young children seem to learn a language faster simply because they require fewer words to sound proficient. It might be fairly quick for a person of any age to acquire the vocabulary of a 4-year-old. However, if you're not four, that level of language won't sound very proficient.

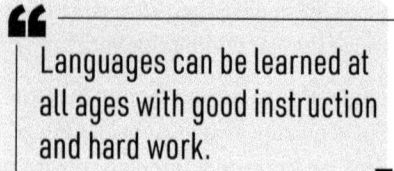

Languages can be learned at all ages with good instruction and hard work.

The reality is that languages can be learned at all ages with good instruction and hard work. There is no evidence to suggest otherwise.

Misconception #2: It Takes 1–2 Years to Learn a New Language

Most people realize that learning a new language takes time. But many people might not realize just how long it takes. Cummins (2000), a prominent researcher on childhood language acquisition through schooling, developed the notions of BICS (basic interpersonal communication skills, or social language) and CALP (cognitive academic language proficiency). According to Cummins, BICS is acquired fairly quickly over the course of 1–2 years. CALP, however, may take 5–7 years. This is thought to be true for adults as well as children. McHugh et al. (2007) estimate that adult immigrants need roughly 6 years of English learning support to pass a naturalization test or be able to begin postsecondary education.

The important thing to remember is that it takes a very long time to fully acquire an additional language, even with good language instruction and opportunities to use the language. It's not a simple or quick task at any age. How long a person of any age will take to reach full proficiency will depend on many factors, including language distance (the level of similarity or difference between the home language and the new language), starting proficiency level, amount of exposure, and opportunities to use the language.

Misconception #3: The More Time People Spend in a New Language Context, the More Quickly They Learn the Language

It takes a long time to learn a language. But can the process be quicker with more exposure? To a certain extent, yes. If a person has minimal input in the target language, they will not learn quickly, and may not gain any real proficiency. Unfortunately, this is a reality that is all too common in foreign language classrooms around the world. When students have only a few hours in the foreign language per week, language acquisition suffers. However, the opposite isn't necessarily true, either: that *more* input is always better. Consider the following:

- **Brain fatigue:** There is a limit on the brain's capacity to absorb new information, including new language. What is that limit for each learner?
- **Home language:** Home language skills play an important role in SLA; higher home language skills have been shown to result in easier and faster SLA. What role does the home language play in acquiring a new language in any given English learning context?
- **Emotional factors:** Krashen's affective filter hypothesis says that a person's general emotional state affects language learning, either facilitating or hindering it. Is there a point at which the continued immersion in a new language becomes frustrating, raising the affective filter, and limiting second language acquisition?

These are not easy questions to answer. But they do highlight some reasons why more immersion in a new language might not always be better. This is especially true in contexts where the home language may not be sufficiently valued.

 Any approach that is based on the unfounded belief that the target language is more important and which results in the loss or lack of development of the home language should be questioned.

Misconception #4: Some People Are Good Language Learners and Some Are Not

Language aptitude tests typically don't take into account the multitude of factors that can contribute to learning a language, and people have varied skills and characteristics that affect that learning in different ways. For example, a person might be weak in sound discrimination, which might result in a lower score on a language aptitude test. But that same person might work hard at forming relationships with speakers of the new language and have a high willingness to communicate, and this would likely help to overcome any deficit in sound discrimination. Some of the characteristics that can positively affect language learning include:

- **Tolerance of ambiguity:** the ability not to fixate on unfamiliar language but attempt to get the gist of something that is read or heard
- **Willingness to communicate:** the effort to engage in communication even when lacking some of the words and structures that are needed
- **Search for patterns:** looking at language as a puzzle and seeing patterns and connections
- **Sound discrimination:** the ability to hear minute differences in sounds, intonation, stress, or tone
- **Outgoing personality:** enjoyment in meeting and connecting to others, even when there may be a language barrier
- **Love of reading:** enjoyment in reading, even in a new language
- **Interest in music, TV, movies, video games, and other technology:** willingness to try to understand new languages that these activities introduce
- **Interest in a location or culture that uses the target language:** desire to get to know a different culture and people

(Read more about some of these and other potential characteristics that can affect language acquisition under "Learner Differences" in Chapter 3.) It is dangerous to conclude that a person would be a "poor language learner" on the basis of aptitude tests or anecdotal evidence. Most individuals who are motivated and who have appropriate resources and instruction are able to learn a new language.

Misconception #5: Language Students Can Use What They Are Taught

It's often assumed that language students should be able to retain the words and grammar that they learn in class and apply these when they are actively using the new language. However, there are two conditions necessary for both remembering new language and being able to actively use it.

First, the language being taught must be at the student's proficiency level. To illustrate, let's say a teacher decides to teach beginners the past perfect verb tense—a complex verb tense in English. Even if the methods and teaching skills are good, the students will not acquire this language because it is too advanced for them. They might be able to memorize rules for forming the tense, but they will not be able to use it.

Second, new language must be used multiple times, in context, and for real communicative purposes before it is remembered. It is unrealistic to introduce a new word, have students memorize it and define it, and then expect that they will use it correctly. Using new language requires many opportunities for meaningful and authentic repeated use, which we will learn more about in Chapter 4.

These misconceptions are important for teachers to understand for two reasons. First, students may believe many of them and may benefit from gaining a more accurate picture of language acquisition. Second, teachers should base their instruction not on popular beliefs but on what we know about language acquisition from the research that we have.

Eight Key Concepts

The theories and research that have emerged in the field of SLA point to eight key concepts that are helpful in understanding how a new language is acquired:

1. **Input:** What kind of language do learners need to receive (read and listen to)?
2. **Output:** What kind of language do learners need to produce (speak and write)?
3. **Interaction:** How does interaction affect language learning?
4. **Fluency:** What is fluency and how is it developed?
5. **Natural sequence:** In what order should students learn specific words and structures?
6. **Language focus:** How much time should students spend focusing on specific language forms?
7. **Stress:** How does stress affect language acquisition?
8. **Time:** How much time does it take to learn a language?

These concepts are drawn from the previously mentioned theories and serve to correct some of the misconceptions discussed.

1. Input

One cannot learn a language without being exposed to it. This exposure, or input, comes through listening and reading. However, what is heard and read must be comprehensible. We cannot acquire language that we don't understand. Figure 1 illustrates the notion of comprehensible input as a person climbing a ladder. A person can only access the next rung up, just as a person can only utilize language input that is just above their current level. (If you recall, Krashen, 1977, calls this level "i+1".)

Some experts (e.g., Nation & Newton, 2020) suggest that 5% is the ideal percentage of new language for understanding. In other words, if we already understand 95% of a text, we are able to comprehend the remaining 5%. Likewise, in oral language, if we can understand 95% of what we hear, we can reach to understand the new 5% from context. But comprehensibility alone is not enough. Input should also be meaningful and engaging. That is, it should give us real information that we are interested in knowing.

FIGURE 1: The theory of comprehensible input means that an individual can only utilize language input that is just above their current level.

Comprehensible input

★ = i + 1

Take Note — The use of visuals, real items, hands-on activities, cooperative learning, facial expressions, and actions can aid comprehension as a person reaches up to the "next rung," or a slightly higher level of language.

Of course, sometimes people are exposed to a lot of language that isn't comprehensible, and they still learn the language. When this happens, it's possible that the learner has consciously or subconsciously filtered out the language that they didn't understand. Such successes are the exception; for many, the stress of struggling to understand a lot of language that is beyond their level results in fatigue, loss of motivation, and ultimately failure in SLA.

2. Output

Input is the first necessary condition for language acquisition. Most people, however, don't just want to comprehend a new language: They want to speak it. They may also want to be able to write it. In other words, they want to be able to produce output.

When a person is just beginning to learn a language, it may be helpful to provide them with a silent period—a period of time to just listen and read in the new language before being expected to produce it. Some language teaching approaches are built around this premise, valuing reception (input) before production (output). In other situations, though, language learners are expected to speak and write in the new language from very early on. Some learners do well with this "pushed output," while others would benefit from a more flexible approach, allowing them to begin speaking when they are ready.

Output plays a key role in SLA because it gives a learner an opportunity to find out how much they know (Swain, 1985). Using the new language draws attention to word forms, grammatical structures, and other language features, providing learners with opportunities to test, confirm, and modify their output.

The amount of output that is needed may depend on cultural, contextual, and personal factors. Language can be acquired by those who are shy and reluctant to speak, for example, and in contexts where students are not expected or allowed to speak much in class. However, there may be delays in productive language development if students don't have sufficient opportunities to actively use language in meaningful communication.

3. Interaction

Language acquisition should be a relational process. Interaction—for example, making a new friend, asking directions to the subway, exchanging emails telling about families—is often a cornerstone of successful language acquisition. Though computer programs, apps, videos, or TV can provide some language input, the input that comes through human interaction has been found to involve different parts of the brain, facilitating increased neurological connections. Interestingly, it can be just as beneficial to interact with other learners as it is to interact with teachers or fluent speakers. Research confirms that hearing mistakes doesn't necessarily make a person more likely to make those mistakes, as long as there is also sufficient opportunity to hear correct forms.

That said, the amount and type of interaction for optimal language acquisition is not yet defined. For example:

- How do language classroom simulations compare to real contexts where learners are interacting with proficient speakers?
- What truly makes interaction meaningful and engaging?
- Do reluctant speakers ever need to be pushed into interaction?

We do not yet have enough research to answer questions like these.

4. Fluency

Successful language learners have fluency: There is a great deal of language readily accessible in their brains because it has been learned to the point of automaticity. Repeated hearing and use of words and phrases has resulted in the learner's processing of these language items automatically, with very little thought or strain.

Fluency is developed through repetition. However, repetition needs to be meaningful. Repeating "What is your name?" 10 times after the teacher is boring and demotivating, but asking 10 different people their names while filling in a survey about your classmates on the first day of class isn't boring, because it's meaningful.

When fluency is the goal, learners should be using words and structures that they already know. Fluency is built by using language that you already understand, over and over again. Fluency isn't limited to speaking, but is needed in all four domains: reading, writing, speaking, and listening:

- *Speaking fluency* is when speech is produced at a normal speed, without pauses that hinder communication.
- *Listening fluency* is when comprehension can easily keep pace with what the other person is saying.
- *Reading fluency* is when we don't need to reread sentences to understand them.
- *Writing fluency* is when words flow fairly effortlessly from the pen or keyboard.

Though we understand repetition is necessary to build fluency, there are still questions about the best ways to utilize repetition in ELT. For example:

- Is repetition through songs and chants as effective as it is through conversations?
- Can talking to oneself build fluency?
- Are timed repetition tasks helpful?

 The key to fluency is abundant repetition, but to repeat the input and output in a way that is authentic and meaningful.

5. Natural Sequence

Language is learned in a somewhat predictable sequence. For example, when we first begin learning a language, we expect to learn things like colors and names for everyday items, not complex verb tenses. We have an intuitive sense that simple nouns and adjectives come before abstract grammar constructions.

One frequent reason for lack of progress in language acquisition is the failure to match language content to the learner's level. When a language learner struggles through a difficult text, looking up many words and failing to grasp the main idea in the process, the text is not at the right reading level. Just as we saw in Figure 1, the learner cannot move up the ladder because the language of the text is too difficult.

Sometimes a teacher proceeds through a course book, moving on to new lessons whether or not previous lessons have been learned. When this happens, content can quickly become out of sync with the learner's language level. This can also happen if the language learner believes that "more and harder" is better and fails to realize that struggling through language tasks significantly above their level is not very helpful in SLA.

The opposite can happen as well: The content can lag behind learner progress. Sometimes this happens because of poorly designed curricula, where the same basic language elements are taught year after year. If language study isn't continually pushed into that next 5% of unknown language, language acquisition can slow down or stop.

Though most people acknowledge the logic of a natural order in language acquisition, it's much less certain what, precisely, that order is. Even if it were possible to outline a specific order in which most learners acquire certain words and structures, the process would still be affected by both individual and contextual factors. For example, for a young child just beginning school, initial vocabulary sets might include names of animals. But an adult immigrant needing to quickly be able to pass a driver's test in a new country might learn complex language about driving rules long before learning names of animals. So, understanding natural sequence is important as a guiding theory, but it does not translate into a concrete, foolproof curriculum for language learning.

6. Language Focus

Language acquisition occurs mainly through exposure to and meaningful use of the language: input and output. However, as learners use language, it's sometimes helpful to focus on language forms. Such focus might include looking closely at a verb tense, a word ending, a tricky sound, or a discourse feature.

Because this kind of study is often overused, it's important to remember that not all language features need to be studied in this way. If a language learner understands a language construction and uses it correctly, there may never be any need for them to learn the grammar rule behind it. Language focus is not essential for language acquisition: Most people use their home language perfectly well, even though few can explain the grammar of that language without specifically studying it. However, for teen and adult learners, there are usually parts of the new language that are confusing, and actively studying those elements may bring clarity and understanding. The key is to ensure that this kind of study remains only a small part of ELT in most contexts.

However, there isn't just one way to leverage language focus for the purpose of furthering overall language acquisition. In some contexts, language learners begin with many hours—and even years—in "language focus" classrooms. Such is the case in many language classrooms where classes consist mostly of grammar, vocabulary, and reading/writing exercises. When given an opportunity to use language for real communication, students from these contexts may fare poorly at first. However, when all that grammar and vocabulary begins to be activated through real, meaningful language use, they may do quite well. The language that they learned passively can become activated and usable.

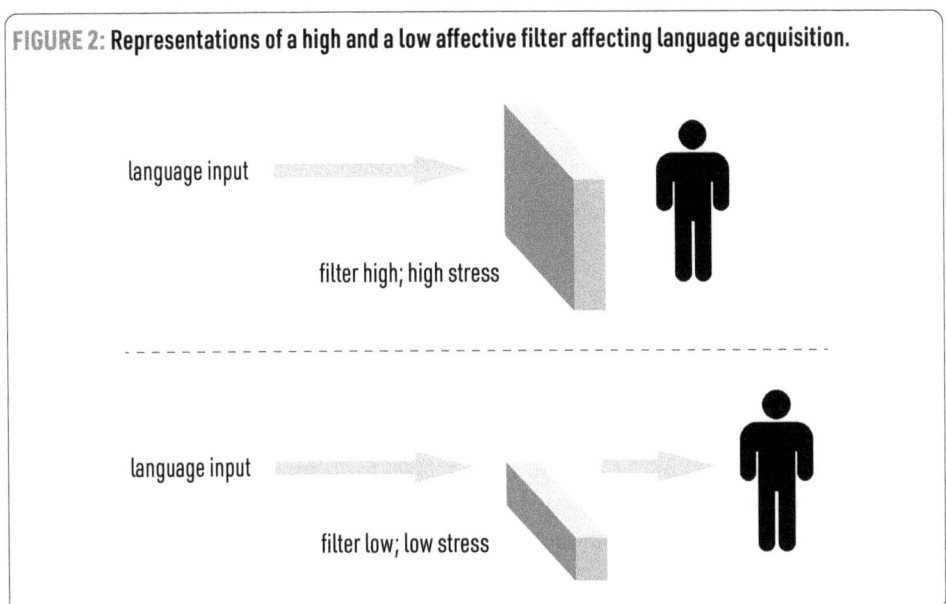

FIGURE 2: Representations of a high and a low affective filter affecting language acquisition.

7. Stress

Krashen (1981) proposed the concept of an **affective filter**. This filter is a number of variables, such as motivation, self-confidence, and stress, that contribute to SLA; when the filter is high (because of high stress, leading to low motivation and self-confidence), SLA is hindered. When it's low (because of low stress, leading to high motivation and self-confidence), SLA is improved (see Figure 2). Brain research has now confirmed this theory. Bailey and Pransky (2013) suggest that cognitive overload can easily occur in language learning contexts and that this causes stress and reduces language acquisition. Here are a few other known stressors in language acquisition:

- ➤ expectations of language performance that are beyond the learner's current ability
- ➤ fears of making mistakes in the classroom
- ➤ inappropriate tests
- ➤ the sheer mental, physical, and emotional fatigue that sometimes accompanies learning a new language

All of these can raise the affective filter, making it difficult to learn language effectively.

 **Take Note** — Language learning is difficult at times, and successful language learners persevere through those times. However, it's important to recognize that difficulty and stress are not the same thing. Stress doesn't add anything of value to language acquisition. Challenge is good, but stress is not. Removing stress can only positively impact language acquisition.

8. Time

The last key concept provides the reminder that it takes a long time to learn a new language. Some estimates place active language learning time at around 2,000 hours to reach intermediate to advanced proficiency. Other studies identify 1–2 years as the time it takes to learn social language, and 5–7 years as the time it takes to acquire academic or professional language. Even more time may be needed if the target language is vastly different from students' home language and other language(s).

Just as important as the amount of time devoted to language acquisition is the strategic investment of that time (Brown & Lee, 2015). Sometimes, a lot of work is done and a lot of time put in, but it's not the kind of work that is likely to result in real communicative competence. For example, hours spent filling out grammar worksheets will likely not result in nearly as much SLA as if those same hours were spent reading an interesting story or talking with someone in the target language.

Because learning a new language is a commitment of years, not weeks or months, it's helpful to approach the task as a lifelong learner. The more a language learner can build in long-term habits and lifestyle choices that include the new language, the more successful SLA will be.

Chapter Summary

This chapter has introduced theories of first and second language acquisition, including misconceptions and key concepts about how people learn new languages. Here are some key points in this chapter:

- First and second language acquisition are alike in some ways, but have some important differences.
- Children and adults have different strengths and challenges when learning a new language.
- Success in learning a new language is dependent on having sufficient opportunity to use a new language for real and meaningful communication.
- People of all ages can acquire a new language when there is
  - sufficient input
  - opportunity for output
  - meaningful interaction using the language with others
  - opportunity for repetition, to develop fluency
  - appropriate pacing and sequencing of language to be learned
  - some language instruction
  - low stress
  - sufficient time

There is solid evidence that language is not acquired by just memorizing words and grammar rules, and other similar decontextualized activities. Language must be used for real communication through reading, writing, speaking, and listening for acquisition to take place. The remaining chapters in this book show how these theories and concepts of SLA can be put into practice in effective ELT.

CHAPTER 3

Addressing Difference: Considering Individual Contexts, Students, and Teachers

English language teaching (ELT) varies a great deal for a great variety of reasons: different contexts and cultures, learner differences (even when contexts and cultures are similar), and teacher differences (because of individual characteristics and because of context and culture). Different contexts and cultures encourage different teacher roles in the classroom and different approaches to teaching a English.

Context Differences

Some traditional ways of distinguishing English learning contexts have to do with the location in which English is being learned (this distinction is reflected in the terms "English as a second language" and "English as a foreign language"), the type of instruction, and the purpose of learning English. Here are some commonly acknowledged English-learning contexts:

Place-Based Contexts

- ➤ **English as a foreign language (EFL):** This refers to English learning in countries that do not use English as a primary language. For example, Germany's national language is German, and Japan's national language is Japanese. In these countries, English is taught and learned as a foreign language in many primary, secondary, and university contexts.

- **English as a second language (ESL):** This term is often used in countries where English is a primary language. For example, English is the dominant language in Australia. Those learning English in Australia acquire it as a second language. In these contexts, the term *ESL* is often used even when English is actually a student's third or fourth language.

Instruction-Based Contexts

- **English-medium general education:** Bilingual, multilingual, or immersion school settings can be found across the globe at all levels of schooling: preschool, primary, secondary, and university. When English is being acquired as an additional language through academic instruction, specific strategies and techniques are needed that are different from those used for language-specific teaching.

- **Language schools and programs:** There are schools and programs that only teach language. Some may teach multiple languages, and others might only teach one. Many of these are private schools, though some language programs are government supported. Language schools might have evening and weekend classes for adults; after-school programs for children; and short, intensive programs during vacation periods.

- **Online instruction:** The teaching of English remotely has seen tremendous growth over the past decade. It truly is "borderless" language instruction, as teachers and students can connect from anywhere around the globe. Remote English instruction can be real time (through live video) or asynchronous (occurring through recorded video and a discussion board, messaging platform, or email).

Purpose-Based Contexts

- **English for specific purposes (ESP):** Some fields of study or work have specialized language, and programs and courses are sometimes designed to teach this language specifically. For example, a course called Business English might focus on the language of international trade, commerce, or finance, and a course called English for Hospitality might focus on concepts of importance in the hotel and tourism industries.

- **English in the workplace:** Sometimes, employers provide English classes at the place of employment. These classes can have a variety of purposes. They might be providing specialized language, as in ESP programs. However, they may be providing basic English instruction to help workers communicate and to help them understand responsibilities and benefits. For example, an ESL program in a Levi Jeans factory in

Canada helps students understand their employee benefits. And a basic English program in Bali is provided by a restaurant owner for his workers to help them as they interact with tourists.

> **English for academic purposes (EAP):** English is often learned for the purpose of academic study. In primary through high school education in English-medium schools, for example, a main goal of acquiring English is for the learning of content. Likewise, intensive English programs in universities teach academic English to equip students with the English skills they will need throughout their university coursework.

These diverse contexts stem from different learning goals, and they each result in differences in the roles of teachers and students in the classroom, and different kinds of assessment and measurements of success.

Cultural Differences

In many language acquisition contexts, language and culture are intertwined. Aspects of culture are acquired along with language, and communication skills are enhanced through focused attention to culture learning. For example, when a person moves to a new country and learns the language of that country, they will also be learning the cultural norms governing the use of the words and phrases that they are learning. Often, word to word translation isn't accurate or useful. Cultural knowledge is needed to translate ideas, not just words. For example, the English question "How are you?" is a typical greeting, and often not a request for information about one's health. If directly translated into Indonesian, however, this would be an inquiry about one's health, not a greeting. Furthermore, an Indonesian greeting comparable to "How are you" in English is "Where are you going?" If this is directly translated into English, it becomes not a greeting, but a question about one's destination. Language can provide a way to express culture, and culture often affects how people use language.

The relative importance of culture-learning within ELT depends on context. Sometimes, the impact of culture will be minimal. For example, a person learning English in an EFL setting to communicate with others who are also using it as a foreign language may have little need to understand the culture of English speakers in a distant country. Additionally, it may be fine for these learners to use English in ways that reflect their own cultures, even if those ways are different from that of English-speaking cultures.

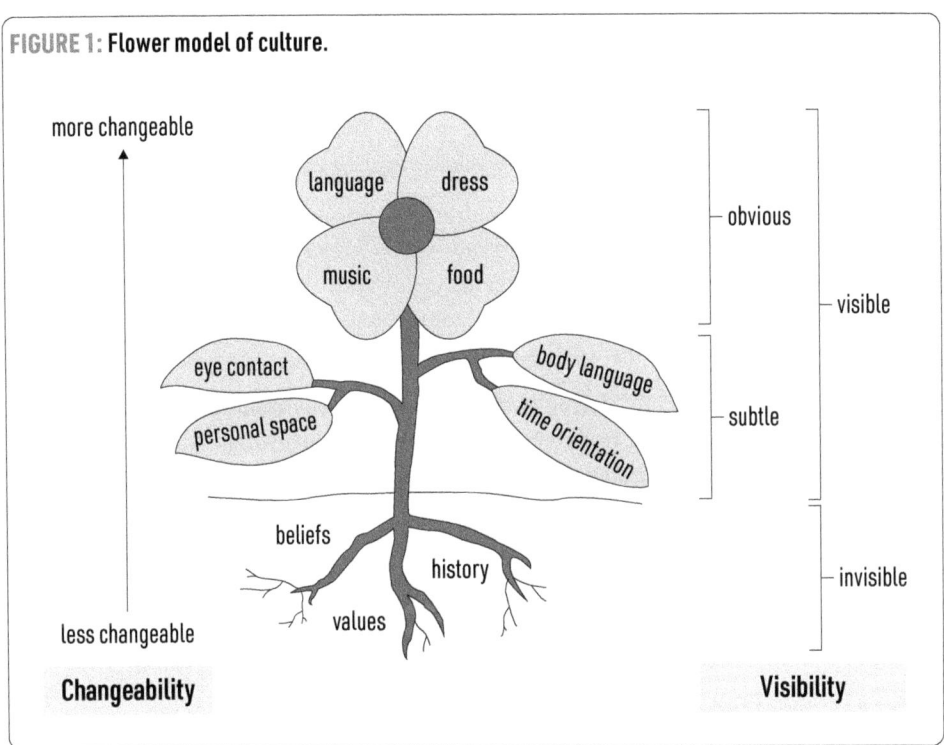

FIGURE 1: Flower model of culture.

However, in many ELT contexts, culture learning is an important component of language learning. For example, a multilingual learner of English (MLE) in English-speaking Canada is living in the new culture and therefore needs to learn about such things as holidays, typical types of dialogues, and common gestures. A student in Brazil might envision traveling to Great Britain for studies, and might have a British teacher at their English school in Brazil. A student in Morocco might be in an English program to prepare them for working in the hospitality industry. In each of these situations, it can be helpful for learners to acquire an understanding of some elements of the English-speaking culture whose English they are learning.

When culture is identified as a necessary learning goal alongside the learning of language, it's important to understand the complex nature of culture, as illustrated in the Flower Model of Culture (Figure 1). It's easy to identify visible signs of culture, such as food and dress (illustrated by the petals of the flower). It's much harder to grasp the different belief systems (illustrated by the roots) that can impact how people communicate. For example, when an English student doesn't ask questions even though they have sufficient English to do so, and they have legitimate questions to ask, it could be because of a belief that asking a question implies the teacher has not explained something well. Their failure to ask questions communicates respect in their own culture, but lack of engagement in the teacher's culture.

This illustrates the importance of viewing culture as two-way learning. The student does need to learn the cultural norms that are typically followed by speakers of the new language. In the example, that is looking the speaker in the eyes to show attention. However, the teacher also needs to learn about the student's culture, and what the student is intending to communicate by not looking the teacher in the eyes.

Table 1 provides examples of differing cultural norms. On the companion website (www.tesol.org/ELTBasics) there is a worksheet version of this chart, which teachers may want to use in their own contexts to engage learners in understanding how cultures that they interact with may differ.

TABLE 1. Two Examples of Differing Cultural Norms

Context	Cultural Norm		
	Noon Meal (Petal)*	Body Language (Leaf)*	Communication Values (Roots)*
United States	Sandwich, salad, soup, or other lighter foods.	Shake hands upon first meeting; stand at a distance in conversation.	Written communication is valued; it provides a record of communication.
Brazil	Biggest meal of the day, often with rice, beans, and meat.	May embrace or "air kiss" on first meeting; stand close for conversation.	Oral communication is valued; it provides more interaction and room for negotiation.

Note: Petal, leaf, and roots refer to the visibility levels of the signs of culture in Figure 1.

All ELT contexts can provide opportunities for learning about other cultures. Certainly, when students represent diverse cultures, or when students and teacher are from different cultures, the ELT classroom should be characterized by respect, value, and support for all cultures in the classroom. Even when students and teacher share the same culture, learning a new language often provides opportunities for learning about cultures associated with that language. Language study may also bring in readings and other materials from other cultures. In short, the ELT classroom can be rich with culture-learning opportunities for teachers and students, and teachers would do well to foster this kind of learning through course materials and activities.

Learner Differences

All learners are unique, and their individual combination of differences impacts language acquisition. Some learners may have exceptional needs. For example, they may experience learning difficulties or may have physical needs requiring accommodations in the classroom. Exceptionalities should be acknowledged and addressed in appropriate ways to facilitate learning.

Learners also may vary considerably in their prior schooling. Immigrant language learners may be highly trained professionals or they might not have learned to read and write in their home language. When literacy needs to be developed, that affects ELT goals considerably. An ideal program would include the development of home language literacy alongside the development of literacy in English.

All language learners need the experiences and conditions discussed in Chapter 2. However, how learners interact with and process these experiences and conditions can vary widely. Here are some of the learner differences that most affect second language acquisition (SLA):

- motivation
- risk-taking
- willingness to communicate
- tolerance of ambiguity
- learning and memory
- sound discrimination

Motivation

Motivation is essential for a task as long and complex as acquiring a new language. Motivation can stem from a desire to integrate into a new culture and build relationships through a new language, or it can be more practical, such as the need to use a new language for work or study. For a few individuals, a love of languages, or of the specific language being learned, provides enough motivation for language acquisition. Some believe that if a person is sufficiently motivated, not much else is needed. Time and again this belief is proven false when highly motivated individuals lose their motivation because of poor language instruction. Motivation is important, but it alone is far from sufficient for SLA.

Risk-Taking

Learning a new language involves using basic and rudimentary language at first, and it involves making mistakes. Many people find it uncomfortable to repeatedly make mistakes, and this feeling may lower their willingness to take risks using the language. When a person is unwilling to take risks, they won't use the language as much, and language acquisition may suffer. A person who perhaps is naturally easygoing and not too concerned about how they sound may acquire English more easily because they are not afraid to use the new language, even in a very basic and imperfect way.

If a person isn't a natural risk-taker, pushing them to take risks beyond their comfort level isn't likely to be helpful and may do nothing more than increase stress, which raises their affective filter (see "Stress" under "Eight Key Concepts" in Chapter 2). If the classroom remains a low-stress, supportive environment, a student may grow in their ability to take more risks as language proficiency increases.

Willingness to Communicate

A person who is eager to communicate an idea will use multiple means of communication, including gestures, reformulations, writing out words, translanguaging, and more. This willingness to communicate can result in the listener providing the language that is needed, or filling in the gaps, resulting in increased language learning. When success is measured by effective communication rather than metrics related to accuracy, an MLE may also be more willing to take risks, because it's easier to be successful.

Willingness to communicate is affected by personality and culture. Just as people differ in introversion and extroversion, cultures also differ in the types and quality of communication that are acceptable in different contexts. In some circumstances, using gestures and a note pad for written words might be not only acceptable but also entertaining. In others, it might be seen as inappropriate.

Tolerance of Ambiguity

Tolerance of ambiguity refers to language that is heard or read. Some learners find it difficult to move past an unfamiliar word in a reading. Tolerance of ambiguity can change, depending on the context. Precise understanding may be needed in some conversations and readings, and not in others. If an MLE is studying to take their driver's license exam, for example, a low tolerance of ambiguity can serve them well, as they will need to fully understand all the language on the exam. However, in general, high tolerance of ambiguity is a helpful quality in learning a new language.

When the topic of a conversation or reading is one that is familiar, a person may be more tolerant of ambiguity because they are more able to predict and understand the content. For someone with low tolerance of ambiguity, even if they might be able to get the gist of a reading without knowing a specific word, they are bothered by the unknown word and feel compelled to look it up, disrupting their reading. In listening, this lack of tolerance for ambiguity has an even more disruptive effect. When we listen to someone speak and get stuck on a single word or phrase, the person continues speaking, but our listening stops. Building tolerance of ambiguity can help a language learner continue to listen, even with partial understanding.

Learning and Memory

Language acquisition occurs mainly through the exposure to and meaningful use of language, not memorization of words and grammar rules. However, there are times when memory tasks can be useful. Most people need to actively and conscientiously work on learning and remembering many new words when they begin to learn a new language. Whether one labels items around the house, uses flash cards, or invents chants and games to aid memorization, this active and focused learning is usually a part of the early language acquisition process. At later stages, learners may need to memorize verb conjugations or noun endings.

The important thing to remember is that though the ability to commit words and grammar rules to memory can be a helpful part of the language acquisition process, memorized language still must be transferred into active language use to have real value. If this occurs, then the memorized language can lead to real communication, and the memorization of grammar rules can provide the ability to self-monitor language use during real interactions, resulting in greater accuracy.

Sound Discrimination

A final learner characteristic that can contribute to language acquisition is the ability to hear, produce, and remember new sounds. This characteristic might not have great significance if English and the home language share similar phonology, but it can be a very important one when the two languages sound very different from each other. Because the effect of sound discrimination on SLA is so different depending on the similarities between the native and target languages, it's dangerous to use this characteristic as a predictor of language acquisition success. Language aptitude tests that focus on sound discrimination don't take into account the fact that sounds are more easily heard and understood in context than in isolation, and when spoken by a real person versus heard on a recording. So, while sound discrimination can be a significant factor in SLA, it must be considered alongside other factors.

Teaching Differences

Teacher roles

Teachers assume different roles in the classroom. What kind of role a teacher adopts can depend on many different factors, including culture, teacher education, type of content, student needs, and personal choice. Two opposing but general teacher roles are sometimes called "transmission" and "facilitation" (see Figure 2).

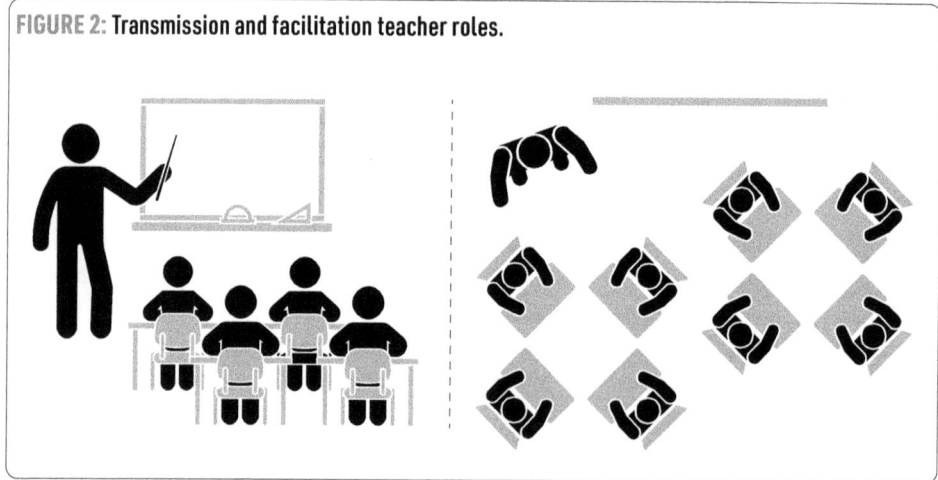

FIGURE 2: Transmission and facilitation teacher roles.

Transmission role

The transmission role casts the teacher as the source of information. In this type of teaching, it's the teacher's job to know the content and transmit it to the students. It's the students' job to learn the content and recite it back on tests. Teachers often transmit the content through lectures. They might also provide content through textbooks and worksheets. This style of teaching is also known as "teacher centered" and is sometimes called a "traditional" way of teaching.

Facilitation role

The facilitation role, in contrast, focuses on students' learning. Though the teacher still needs to know the content, their main role isn't transmitting that content, but, rather, helping students to learn it. This is sometimes called a "student-centered" approach to teaching. When the teacher is acting in a facilitative role, they design learning activities that they believe will result in students learning the content. Such activities might include pair and small group work and interactive classroom activities, such as games, simulation of real-world activities, and project-based learning.

Because students of the English language need to actively use English for real communication, a facilitative role is often the most helpful in ELT. However, it's important to recognize that ELT contexts are diverse, and numerous factors impact the role that the teacher adopts. For example, when considering the local culture (including student expectations) and national exams, a transmission approach might be needed for some of the instruction. Well-equipped teachers are those who can be flexible in their approach, changing teaching roles as needed to both respect culture and also provide instruction that will result in student learning.

Language Teaching Approaches

Different words are used to talk about the ways that teachers teach and the activities through which students are expected to learn. An overarching term that is often used in such discussions is *methodology*. However, methods are chosen based on the approach that is taken. An approach is a perspective, or a set of beliefs, about how students will best learn or acquire a new language. This perspective then drives the selection of methods, which then leads to the use of specific activities in which students will engage (see Figure 3).

Approaches to language teaching can fall under three broad categories:

- Language based
- Communication based
- Content based

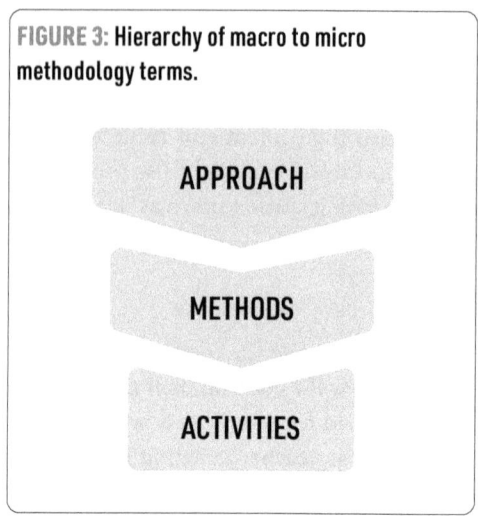

FIGURE 3: Hierarchy of macro to micro methodology terms.

Language-based approaches

Language-based approaches are the most traditional, and often go hand-in-hand with a transmission teaching role. In this type of approach, the main goal is to learn *about* the language. The oldest of this type of approach is called grammar translation and focuses primarily on the written language. Lessons involve learning grammar, memorizing vocabulary, reading and translating texts, and filling out worksheets. There is relatively little focus on what is being communicated through the language.

Historically, when the grammar translation approach proved to be insufficient for real-world communication, the audiolingual method was born. Unlike the grammar-translation method, the audiolingual method focused on oral language. However, the emphasis was still on the language itself. Though real-world communication was a stated goal, its methodology of memorization of dialogues and an emphasis on work done in language labs, listening and repeating, did not always result in the real-world communicative ability that was desired.

Communication-based approaches

Dissatisfaction with the results of language-focused approaches led to an emphasis on communication in language classrooms. Communication-based approaches focus less on perfection in grammar, pronunciation, and other elements of language and more on meaning and achieving success in a communication task. Communicative classrooms are designed to provide opportunities for real, meaningful, and authentic communication, typically through all four domains of speaking, listening, reading, and writing.

In this type of approach, teachers often take a facilitative role. They design classroom activities that provide students with opportunities to use the language for real and purposeful communication. This approach has often been called communicative language teaching. One way in which communicative language teaching has been envisioned in curriculum is through **task-based language teaching**. In this type of curriculum, language acquisition occurs through tasks that students need to accomplish through the language. For example, a student might be tasked with engaging in dialogue to open a bank account through a classroom simulation.

Content-based approaches

A content-based approach shifts the emphasis yet again. The emphasis isn't on the language or the communication but on the content learned through the language. This approach is used in bilingual and language immersion school settings, when language acquisition occurs through content instruction in a new language. For example, when a child in Malaysia speaks Malay at home but goes to an English-medium school where all subjects are taught in English, the child experiences content-based language learning. When her math, science, and history classes are taught in English, she is acquiring English as she is learning those subjects. Similarly, a fluent-English-speaking adult living in France might choose to take a cooking class in French as a way of learning French. The focus would be on the content of cooking, but a byproduct would be learning French.

Some of the labels given to this type of approach include **content and language integrated learning**, **content-based instruction**, and content-based language teaching. Language is sometimes acquired through content instruction in classrooms that provide sheltered instruction. A sheltered classroom is one in which content is delivered in more accessible English, using strategies that help students both learn content and acquire language. One well-known method of planning for such sheltered instruction is SIOP: Sheltered Instruction Observation Protocol.

There are other approaches that are not limited to language teaching, which can also be very useful in developing language through content instruction. Project-based learning is an approach in which students work in groups to complete a project. To complete the project, they must both learn the necessary content and utilize the target language. Problem-based learning is similar, but the students' collaborative goal is to solve a problem. To solve the problem, they must learn content and use language.

Utilizing Multiple Approaches

In many ELT contexts, different approaches are needed at different times and for different purposes. Imagine an EFL secondary classroom in Colombia in which the teacher is teaching a unit on robotics, which she hopes will pique students' interest (Table 2).

TABLE 2. EFL Classroom Teaching Scenario Using Varied Approaches

Classroom Teaching	Teaching Approach
The teacher uses the English language as she teaches about robotics.	Content-based approach
Students are interacting in English in small groups to process their learning and design a robot.	Communication-based approach
From time to time, the teacher addresses errors she hears as students work in groups. (E.g., she notices students' misuse of the pronouns *for* and *to*, and so provides a mini-lesson on this topic.)	Language-focused approach

Well-trained teachers are able to select, use, and integrate approaches to meet the language learning needs.

Chapter Summary

ELT varies around the globe. English teaching and learning is done in many different kinds of schools, within diverse country contexts.

- › The cultures of the students, teacher, and the type of English being taught can impact ELT endeavors in various ways.
- › Probably the most important type of diversity in the classroom is that of the students. Each student has unique strengths and challenges in the language acquisition process.
- › Teachers can take on different roles in the classroom. A facilitative role is most likely to result in students being able to communicate in the new language.
- › There are many different approaches, methods, and strategies that can be used in language classrooms. Teachers should know many of these to best meet the needs of their students through diverse classroom experiences.

The more teachers understand the diversity of the ELT classroom and are able to tailor their teaching to their ELT context and learners, the more successful they will be.

CHAPTER 4

Planning and Teaching English Language Lessons

This chapter gets to the heart of English language teaching (ELT): what happens in the classroom. It begins with an introduction to planning lessons. Core lesson components are introduced, along with some sample lesson outlines. The second half of the chapter addresses teaching lessons, and the essential skills that teachers need to create effective language acquisition experiences for their students.

A Note on This Chapter: Special Cases

The assumption in this chapter is that teachers are in a context where students want to learn to speak English, and where it is also appropriate to integrate all four language skills (listening, speaking, reading and writing) into the lesson.

There are some contexts in which lessons might need to be designed differently because of students' needs and goals. For example, an English class in which the students do not yet have literacy even in their home language might only use visual supports, and might not use written English words and sentences. A class that is focused on preparing students for a college entrance exam might consist mostly of individual reading, writing, and grammar activities, and might not have much emphasis on communication or interaction.

There are many resources for teaching classes focused on specific language skills, such as reading or listening, or specific goals, such as test preparation. A list of resources can be found on the companion website for this book (www.tesol.org/ELTBasics).

Planning Lessons: Lesson Components

Classroom instruction normally begins with planning a lesson. Though it may seem that veteran teachers are able to enter a classroom with little preparation, engaging students in rich activities that foster language learning, these teachers have usually developed their teaching skills over years of conscientious lesson planning. For effective ELT that results in students being able to communicate in their new language, a teacher cannot simply open a workbook and go through the exercises with the students. New teachers need to plan lessons well in order to achieve the goal of student language acquisition.

There are many different lesson planning models. Teacher training programs or schools often have required templates for planning lessons. Sometimes, these templates require many different components, all of which can be helpful in learning to plan a lesson. However, the goal in this chapter is to focus on only the essential elements that are needed to plan a lesson that will result in language acquisition. These are the three essential components of a lesson plan for language acquisition (or "Triple A" Lesson Planning):

1. Aims
2. Activities
3. Assessment

Aims

Every lesson plan for language acquisition begins by asking one question:

> "What language and skills do I want students to learn, practice, and use?"

Aims can go by other names, such as lesson objectives, goals, or targets. Some lesson planning systems use these words in different ways, such as the use of "aims" for long-term goals, and the use of "objectives" for an individual lesson. Whatever it is called, it's important to have language that is aimed for, and to use this goal to direct the choice of class activities. On the journey of language acquisition, aims are

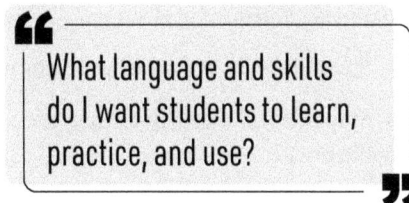

> "What language and skills do I want students to learn, practice, and use?"

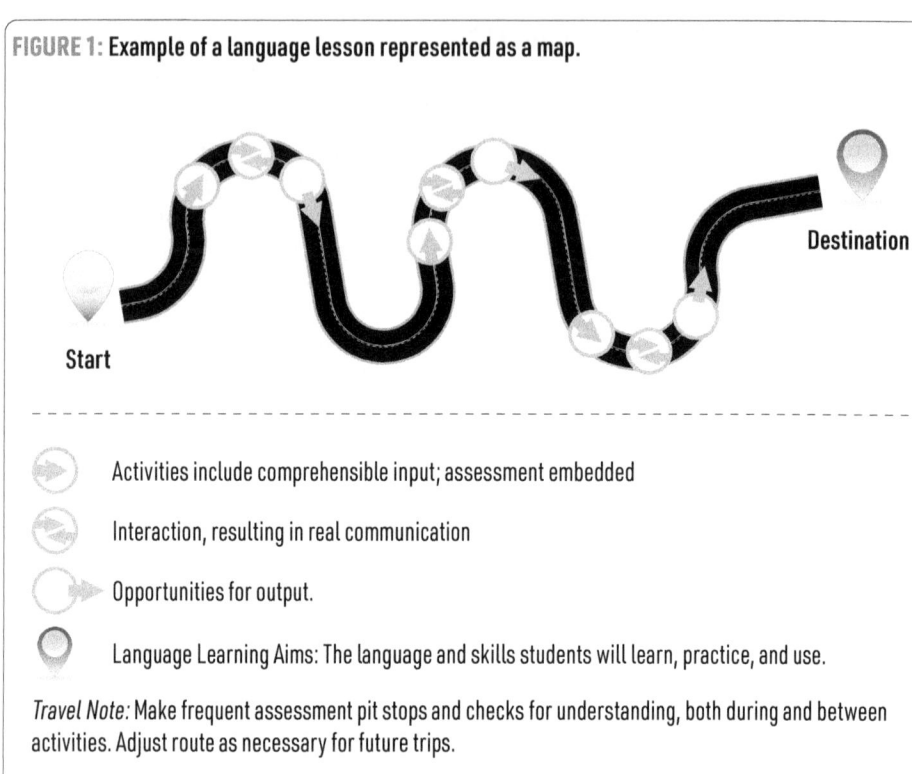

FIGURE 1: Example of a language lesson represented as a map.

- Activities include comprehensible input; assessment embedded
- Interaction, resulting in real communication
- Opportunities for output.
- Language Learning Aims: The language and skills students will learn, practice, and use.

Travel Note: Make frequent assessment pit stops and checks for understanding, both during and between activities. Adjust route as necessary for future trips.

the destination, and activities are the steps you take to get there (see Figure 1). Here are some sample statements of aims, which might also be called lesson objectives:

Example Statement of Aims

➤ Students will use past tense forms when telling what they did last month.

➤ Students will create questions about past activities, using the structure "What did you do on…?"

➤ Students will produce the /th/ (/ð/ and /θ/) sound.

Language lessons often have several aims. For example, the aforementioned example aims could go together in a lesson in which students tell each other about their past activities:

Example Lesson

The teacher begins by showing a calendar of the previous month with three dates highlighted (November 4, 16, and 30). She's written the prompt question ("What did you do on November ___?") on the board and has a student ask her about one of the dates. She answers, "On November 4th, I attended a concert." She then places students in pairs to do the same activity. For increased practice, the teacher then does a survey activity in which students go around the room finding out what each student did on November 4, 16, or 30. Because there is class time left, she then has students work with new partners, reporting what their first partner had done and on which date, thus switching the sentence from first and second person "I/you" statements, to third person "he/she/they" statements while repeatedly practicing the pronunciation aim.

In the example lesson, the teacher accomplishes all three aims with careful planning of activities.

Activities

The teacher's main task at the planning stage is to design instruction that will result in students achieving the lesson aims. When the aims are to help students acquire English through communication, a lesson plan mostly consists of a sequence of activities in which students will interact.

Though it might be necessary to briefly introduce and explain new words or language structures, a common error in ELT is making this introduction and explanation the focus of the lesson. Instead, the focus of the lesson should be on real language use: Often, student understanding of new words and structures will come as they use them—not as teachers explain them.

The concepts of input, interaction, and output can be helpful for selecting activities in which students can use English for real communication. As shown in Figure 2, communicative activities often begin with some type of input—something that the students hear or read. The input must be comprehensible (at the right level for each student). Often, this initial input is followed by some kind of interaction. This could be interaction between teacher and students, or interaction between students in pairs or small groups. The interaction then leads to opportunities for output, in which students speak or write as they use language to communicate.

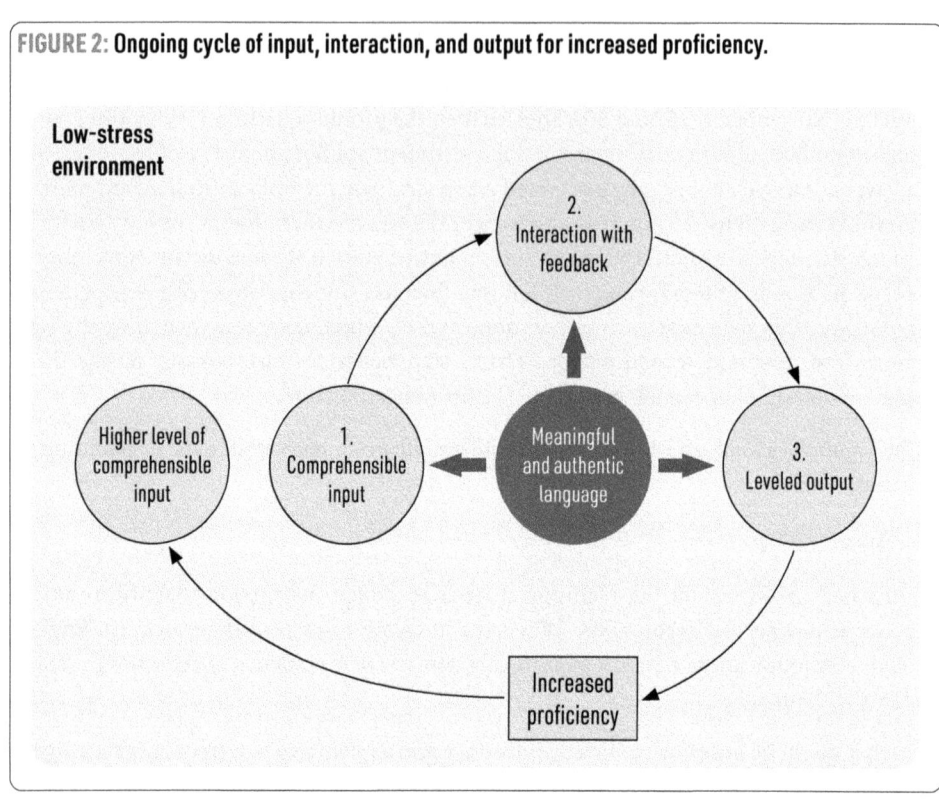

FIGURE 2: Ongoing cycle of input, interaction, and output for increased proficiency.

It's important that input, interaction, and output involve meaningful and authentic language use. In other words, students should be reading, writing, speaking, and listening on topics that are meaningful and interesting to them, and the language used should be authentic: It should be language that they will hear and use in the real world context for which they are learning English.

It's important to remember, as well, that all this communicative language use should occur within an overall environment that is low stress. When students have anxiety about producing language with errors, not getting a good grade, or taking a test for which they don't feel prepared, it inhibits their ability to acquire language. Figure 2 also shows what happens as a result of the input, interaction, and output: Students' language proficiency will increase. At that point, the cycle can begin again, with comprehensible input at a slightly higher level.

Assessment

Instruction should always include ways to determine its effectiveness, and this is often called assessment.

>
> Assessment should be a normal and regular part of English language teaching, and results should impact future instruction.
>

- Have the students achieved the aims of the lesson?
- How do we know?

These are the questions that assessment should answer. Assessment can be as simple as a teacher walking around the room, listening to students as they talk in pairs and keeping a checklist of who has mastered a new structure and who still needs more practice. Assessment can also be much more planned and consequential, such as having students give a final presentation utilizing language learned during the semester.

Assessment should be a normal and regular part of English language teaching, and results should impact future instruction. For example, in the earlier example lesson scenario, the teacher might listen as students work in pairs, noting students' use of correct question forms, past tense forms, and the /th/ (/ð/ and /θ/) sound. If the teacher hears many errors, she will know to plan more activities using these language forms and to provide more assistance during class time. The following sample lesson outlines show some additional examples of how assessment can be naturally incorporated into language lessons. Chapter 5 also further explores different types and purposes of assessment.

Sample Lesson Outlines

Lesson for Beginning-Level Sudents: Family Tree

Note: See the companion website for this book (www.tesol.org/ELTBasics) to view a video of this lesson being taught.

Aims

- Students will use family words (*lower*: brother, sister, father, mother; *higher*: niece, nephew, cousin, in-laws) when asking and answering questions.
- Higher proficiency students will use possessives when asking and answering questions (E.g., "Who is Jay's wife?", "Is Anna Sharon's daughter?")

Activities

Input

1. Show a nuclear family drawing or photo (preferably, your own family). Place word labels on each member of the family, saying each word. Introduce all nuclear family words.

2. Say sentences about family relationships, writing them on the board. (E.g., "Rod is Jan's husband." "Jenna is Jan's daughter.")

3. Ask questions about family relationships, writing them on the board. (E.g., "Who is Rod?", "Who is Jenna's mom?")

Interaction

4. Give student pairs a blank extended family tree (preferably of your own family), with family member's name on pieces of paper that fit in the blanks.

5. Elicit questions from students to learn where the names go. Students ask questions, such as "Who is Jay?" and "Who is Jay's wife?" Students continue asking questions until the family tree is complete.

Output

6. Give each pair a copy of the completed family tree (or have students take a picture of their completed tree). Students remove the names from the tree and place them upside down on their desk. One student turns over a name and asks a question (e.g., "Who is Jay?"). The other student makes a sentence about Jay, referring to the completed family tree (e.g., "Jay is Jan's brother.").

7. Place students in small groups and instruct them to write the names of five family members on a piece of paper to show their group. One student shows their paper, and each other student asks a question about one of the names (e.g., "Who is Miori?"). The student answers each question (e.g., "Miori is my sister.") and then the next student takes their turn.

Assessment

➤ Have student names on a chart and listen as students engage in Step 7. Note whether students are using family words with ease or if they still need more practice.

➤ Listen to the higher proficiency students as they engage in Step 7 to see if they are using possessives accurately or if they need more feedback or practice.

Lesson for Intermediate-Level Students: Vacation Complainers[1]

Aim

➤ Students will produce sentences using the construction "too + adjective + to"

Activities

Input

1. Ask students, "Have you ever visited a nice place, only to hear others complaining? Maybe they complained about the weather or the prices or the hotel." Give an example from your personal experiences: "For example, I recently visited Germany. I enjoyed being in a quaint old town in the wintertime, but I heard someone at the guest house complaining: 'It's too cold to walk around town. The streets are too dark at night to see where you're going. A vehicle is too expensive to rent.'"

2. Point out the "too – adjective – to" construction in each sentence. Help students understand that *too*, unlike *very*, has a negative connotation.

Interaction

3. Place students in pairs. Give each pair a card with a vacation destination on it.

4. Have them write three to five possible sentences like the ones on the board, as if they are a complaining tourist.

Output

5. Have each pair come up and read their sentences aloud. With that information, the class tries to guess the location.

Assessment

➤ As pairs give their sentences, note whether they are using the construction "too ___ to" correctly.

---

1. Adapted from "Adjectives, Adverbs, and Nouns," by J. Dormer, in *New Ways in Teaching Grammar*, edited by C. Rylance and A. Kevech, 2018, pp. 3–4. Copyright 2018 by TESOL Press. Adapted with permission.

Lesson for Advanced-Level Students: Have You Ever?

Aims

- Students will ask and answer questions about experiences and report on a classmate's experiences using present perfect. They will use these structures:
  - Have you ever
  - I / you / they have / haven't ever / have never
  - S/he has / hasn't ever / has never

Activities

Input

1. Say: "I will say three statements about my life. Try to guess which one is not true!" (Make statements using present perfect, e.g., "I haven't ever been to Morocco," "I have gone hang gliding," and "I haven't studied calculus.")

2. Ask students to guess which one is not true. They should make complete sentences, such as "I think you *have* been to Morocco," "I think you *haven't* gone hang gliding," or "I think you *have* studied calculus."

3. Put on the board these sentence starters:
   - Have you ever…. ? No, I have never… / No, I haven't ever…
   - Have you ever….? Yes, I have.

Interaction

4. Have each student think of one question to ask classmates, starting with "Have you ever…". For example:
   - Have you ever milked a cow?
   - Have you ever sailed a boat?
   - Have you ever sung on stage?

Have students go around the room asking their classmates this question. At the end, have students report to the whole class, making statements such as these:

- Only Stephan has milked a cow.
- Patricia and Ali have sailed boats.
- No one has sung on stage.

5. Play "Upset the fruit basket" (see instructions in Ch. 6). The person in the middle should say something they have never done, such as "I have never eaten kimchi. Move if you *have* eaten kimchi." All students who have eaten kimchi must find a new seat, and the person left without a seat is in the middle.

6. Have students write a list of 10 questions such as the ones in Step 4, starting with "Have you ever…". Place students in pairs and have them ask and answer each other's questions. Give students identical cards or pieces of paper to write on. Have students write a list of what their partner has and hasn't done (without writing their partner's name). For example:
   - They have never ridden a horse.
   - They have run in a marathon.
   - They haven't ever played guitar.
   - Collect all the cards and read them one at a time. Students guess who each person is.

Output

7. Have students write paragraphs using one of these prompts:
   - Tell about several things that you haven't done yet, but that you want to do in the future.
   - Tell how you are similar to or different from one of your classmates, in what you have and haven't done.

Assessment

➤ Note students' use of "I haven't ever" and "I've never" in Upset the Fruit Basket. Provide corrective feedback as needed.

➤ Note students' written uses of "They have / they haven't ever / they have never" in the sentences about their partner. Provide individualized feedback as needed.

➤ Assess written use of the targeted structure in their paragraphs.

Teaching Lessons

Planning a good lesson is only a starting point in teaching well. Teachers also need skill in carrying out the plan and responding appropriately to what happens in the classroom. As students interact with others, use English, and ask questions and share ideas, teachers need to respond in ways that not only further language acquisition but also foster a relaxed, enjoyable, and relational environment. There are many resources on teacher skills in the ELT classroom. Some of those are listed on the companion website for this book (www.tesol.org/ELTBasics).

Following are discussions on seven important areas of teacher skill:

1. Teacher talk
2. Setting the tone
3. Grouping
4. Explaining
5. Scaffolding
6. Corrective Feedback
7. Teacher Reflection

1. Teacher Talk

Teachers typically talk a lot. Some of this talk is necessary and helpful. When teachers talk, it can help build relationships with students and also model new language. However, too much teacher talk, and the wrong kind of teacher talk, can limit students' opportunities to engage in using the new language themselves. Here are some things to remember about teacher talk:

1. **Speech should be slow, clear, and well enunciated.** Students have a more difficult time comprehending and reproducing language when teachers speak quickly, connect words, and don't enunciate well so that students can hear all parts of the words and sentences.

2. **Teachers should use natural intonation and volume.** Intonation is a very important feature of language. Students need to hear the natural cadence of English, but at a slower pace. Avoid the common tendency to speak louder to multilingual learners of English (MLEs).

3. **Most teachers need to reduce teacher talk.** When students are beginners, and possibly in an initial silent period, teachers will naturally talk more. This talk should include a lot of repetition of words and phrases. As students progress, it's important that teacher talk be reduced in favor of students speaking; the majority of the class time should consist of activities in which students will use English.

2. Setting the Tone

Figure 2, earlier in this chapter, provides a reminder of the importance of a low-stress environment in the classroom. In many language classrooms, students feel anxious or bored for a variety of reasons. Some common reasons include:

Anxiety

➤ The level of the course materials is too difficult for them, and thus not comprehensible.

➤ They fear the teacher might call on them and they will not be successful in producing the language accurately or giving the correct answer.

➤ They may fear ridicule from other students.

➤ They may be worried about getting a poor grade in the class.

Boredom

➤ The language being learned or the activities are too hard: Students may become inattentive and unwilling to engage in learning.

➤ The language being learned or the activities are too easy: Sometimes students are taught the same language from year to year and are bored because they already know it.

A teacher's first tasks are (1) to ensure that the curriculum and materials are appropriate for the students and (2) to communicate the expectation that students will be engaged, willing to take risks, and supportive of each others' learning. How this is done depends on the context and what is appropriate given the culture, age of students, their prior learning experiences, and other factors.

In most contexts, the tone evolves into one of positivity and encouragement as teachers provide interesting and motivating topics and tasks and communicate enjoyment, affirmation, and supportiveness. Students begin to mirror the teacher's attitudes and actions, and a classroom environment conducive to second language acquisition begins to form.

3. Grouping

Because MLEs need to use language through reading, writing, speaking, and listening, they benefit from many activities in which they are interacting in pairs or small groups. Though whole-class instruction and activities are useful and appropriate at times, students need frequent opportunities to use the language. Here are some tips when grouping students:

- **Prepare students for pair and group work.** Don't assume that they will automatically know what to do or how to interact with each other. If students will be assigned roles, teach and model these roles and the group work expectations.

- **Clearly state what students should do.** Prompts should be specific. For example, "Share what you like to do" is vague. A more effective prompt would specify details, provide structure to the activity, and give examples or sentence frames:

  Example Prompt

  Tell each other three things that you like to do in your free time. Follow this sequence:

  › Student 1: "What do you like to do in your free time?"
  › Student 2: "I like to…."
  › Student 2: "What do you like to do in your free time?"
  › Student 1: "I like to…"

  Do this three times. Write down what your partner says.

- **Clearly state how much time students have, and respect the timer.** A timer can be helpful in keeping students on track. Even if all groups have not finished, it can set an important expectation, letting students know the importance of staying on task. Do make sure the time you set is realistic. When teachers either don't provide enough time or leave students in groups for a long time after the task has been finished, students can feel demotivated due to frustration or boredom. Walking through the exercise yourself and then adding a bit more time can help you plan realistic time limits.

- **Create purposeful groups.** For longer tasks, purposefully create the pairs and small groups rather than having students form their own groupings. This enables you to consider student language levels, personalities, and other factors for maximum effectiveness.

- ► **Consider language level.**
  - › Group students of similar language levels together when you need to provide different activities or resources for different levels. For example, if beginning level students will have an easier text to read than more advanced students, group these students together.
  - › Group students of diverse language levels together when these students can learn from and help each other. For example, students with diverse language levels might speak the same home language, and the MLEs more proficient in English might provide some translation for those less proficient. Even if students don't speak the same language, MLEs with early proficieny might benefit from hearing language at a slightly higher level without being required to use that language yet, and higher level students might benefit from opportunities to explain language structures to other students.

- ► **Consider who needs to speak.** If it's important for all students to talk, pairs are sometimes more effective than small groups because there is an obligation to participate when a student is working with just one other person. If you want to ensure that an MLE with early proficiency has the opportunity to just listen and not speak, small groups are better.

- ► **Build group rapport.** Maintaining the same pairs or groups for several different activities, days, or weeks can increase student comfort level. However, look for any difficulties groups are experiencing, and be willing to change groupings as needed.

4. Explaining

In most ELT contexts, students don't acquire language through explanations, but through use. For example, students don't develop the ability to use past tense "–ed" endings because teachers explain them, but rather because they have many opportunities to use them.

That said, there are limited times in language classrooms when students can benefit from an explanation of a word or grammatical structure. When such explanations are called for, it's important that they be clear, brief, at the students' language level, and followed by usage.

Following is an example of a teacher noticing many students in her class making an error and adjusting her lesson to include a brief explanation to address that error:

Teacher Explanation Example

A teacher notices that many of her students are omitting "–ed" endings when talking about past events. She decides to take a 5-minute break from the communicative activities she has planned to offer an explanation:

> *When we talk about the past, regular verbs have "–ed" on the end. I hear "I walk to school yesterday." Instead, say "I walked to school yesterday."* [Teacher writes this sentence on the board, underlining the "–ed".] *In pairs, add the "–ed" to the verb, and say these sentences:*
>
> › *I (play) soccer last week.*
>
> › *She (work) outside yesterday.*
>
> › *He (look) up a word.*
>
> › *The teacher (point) to the word.*

The teacher then walks around the room, listening to pairs as they produce the sentences, eliciting past-tense endings as needed. After this very brief explanation and practice, the students return to the communicative activity they were engaged in before the explanation and continue sharing about past events.

In this scenario, it might be tempting for a teacher to launch into an explanation of the different sounds of "–ed", which are /t/ as in *worked*, /d/ as in *played*, and the syllable "–ed" as in *pointed*. However, many students don't actually need instruction in these sounds, as they are able to hear and repeat the sounds without direct instruction. If the teacher does hear a student using an incorrect sound, such as saying the word *wor-ked* with two syllables rather than one, then the teacher can simply provide feedback correcting the pronunciation, and the student can quickly return to using language for real communication.

5. Scaffolding

In English language classrooms, a significant part of a teacher's job is providing students with the assistance they need to be able to use progressively more difficult language for meaningful communication. As students make efforts to add new words and structures to their language repertoire, teachers can **scaffold** new language for them in various ways. In other words, the teacher provides some supports to help students effectively use new language. Several types of scaffolds are discussed here. See the companion website for this book (www.tesol.org/ELTBasics) for more types of scaffolds and examples.

Connecting

All lessons should build on previous learning and connect to students' experiences. Rather than expecting that students will make these connections themselves, teachers should build in introductory activities that help students make these connections.

Example Scaffold: Connecting

To introduce a lesson in which students will read about access to clean water, the teacher begins by bringing in water samples for tasting. The teacher also shows pictures of various ways that people get clean drinking water. He then asks students to share with each other how they have gotten clean water in various places where they have lived, inviting them to find another class member who has had the same experience.

The beginning activities in the example help students become interested in the topic and activate background knowledge and experiences that will help them understand and connect to the content.

Preteaching

Sometimes, students benefit from the preteaching of words or concepts prior to a dialogue, discussion, or reading. This is particularly true for essential or key words for a text, and it can be helpful for all students, regardless of proficiency level or home language. When the meanings of words can be illustrated through visuals, synonyms, or quick translations, this can be especially effective.

Example Scaffold: Preteaching

In a lesson on clean water, students will have a reading on access to clean water. The teacher preteaches the words *filter, bacteria,* and *access*. He shows pictures of several different water filters. He then provides the word *germ* as a synonym for *bacteria*. Finally, he says, "Some people have to walk far to get good water." He writes on the board and says "They don't have easy access to water," emphasizing and underlining *access*. He then elicits from students the translation of *access* in their languages, encouraging them to use bilingual dictionaries or electronic translators as needed. One concept, *scarcity*, is too complicated to preteach quickly, so he allows his students to gather the meaning through the reading, from context. Afterward, the teacher conducts a comprehension check to ensure that the concept has been understood.

When words or concepts require longer explanations (e.g., *scarcity* in the preceding example), sometimes students will be able to acquire the meaning through the reading, and this may be more effective than a long, drawn-out explanation at the beginning, but it's important to check for comprehension on any difficult terms that were not pretaught.

Modeling

Modeling is usually helpful when students are first introduced to new language or a new type of task. Teachers might model different types of language used with different interlocutors (different registers); patterns of speech found in tasks, such as introducing someone; or typical dialogues in common contexts, such as shopping or ordering coffee.

Example Scaffold: Modeling

Students are to tell each other about their families using a family photo. The teacher brings in her own family photo and tells students about her own family first, and she writes the new words and structures she uses on the board: *niece* and *nephew*. The teacher provides a visual of her own family tree, pointing and saying, "This is my brother's daughter. She is my niece. Her name is Anna. Anna is my niece."

Modeling tasks so that students have seen exactly what they are to do can decrease the number of questions students ask before getting started and increase students' ability to stay engaged and complete the task.

Demonstrating words on fingers

Addressing words needed, words left out, or word order in short sentences can be done simply by using the fingers.

Example Scaffold: Words on Fingers

A student is trying to produce the sentence "I have a brother," but says "I have brother." The teacher holds up four fingers, connecting the first finger to "I" and the second to "have." He then gestures that the word representing the third finger is missing, moving on to connect the fourth finger to "brother." Now, the student is aware that a word is missing, but still cannot readily produce "a," so the teacher says "a" and demonstrates the sentence using the four fingers. The teacher then gestures for the student to produce the sentence, using their own fingers.

In longer sentences, word order can be shown through words on sticky notes, or on cards laid out on a desk. Sometimes, it can be helpful to color-code words, making all nouns blue and all nouns green, for example.

Sentence frames and starters

Sentence frames and starters are excellent ways to scaffold new language. A sentence frame is essentially a written sentence with blanks, and a sentence starter provides just the beginning of the sentence. Sentence starters can be helpful at higher language levels when students are producing longer sentences.

Example Scaffold: Sentence Frames and Starters

> *Frames:* Students are expected to talk about their family members. The teacher writes on the board, "This _____ my _____." and "These _____ my _____." These sentence frames help students to produce sentences such as "This is my sister" and "These are my nephews."

> *Starters:* The teacher writes on the board, "My favorite pastime is _____." She says, "Complete the sentence with your favorite pastime and a reason. For example, "My favorite pastime is playing sports because it helps me stay healthy."

When sentence frames and starters are specific to a particular lesson or topic and aren't necessary for all students, it can be helpful to write the sentence frames and starters on manila folders. These can be placed in front of students who need the support. They can then be stored with the unit or lesson plan, and pulled out again the next time the teacher teaches that lesson.

Sentence frames and starters can also be more general, used as support for discussion, such as expressing an opinion, comparing and contrasting, agreeing and disagreeing, and so on. These types of frames and starters can be posted on the wall throughout the year for all students (see Figure 3). Here are some examples:

➤ *Expressing an opinion:* I think/believe that _____; In my opinion, _____; Based on my experience, I think _____,

➤ *Comparing and contrasting:* One similarity between _____ and _____ is _____; _____ and _____ are different/similar because _____.

➤ *Agreeing and disagreeing:* I agree/disagree with _____, but/and _____.

FIGURE 3: Example of sentence frames on a classroom wall.

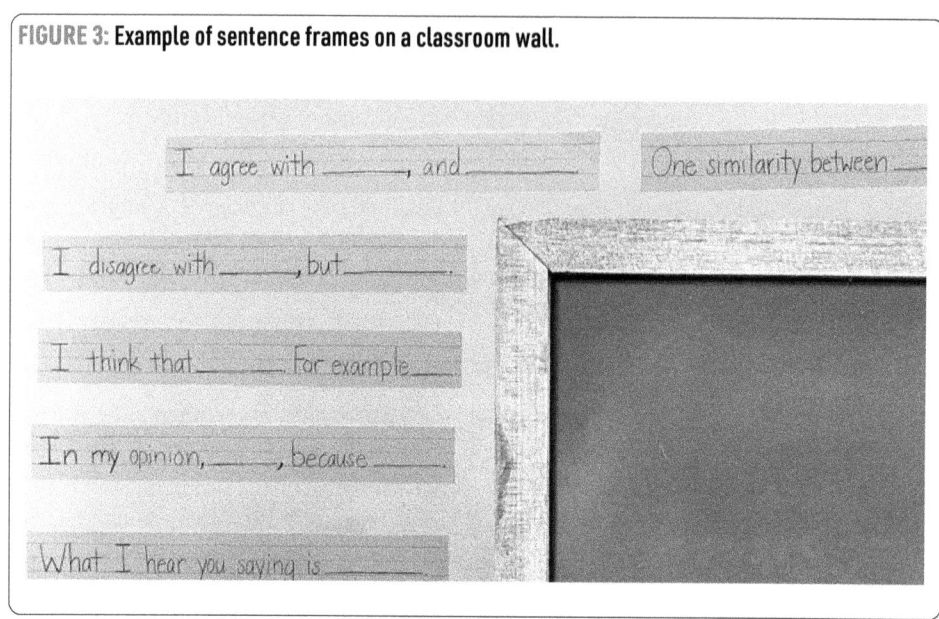

For more examples of sentence frames and starters, see the companion website for this book (www.tesol.org/ELTBasics).

Alternative Texts

If students will be asked to read a challenging text, it can be helpful to provide the same textual information at a lower English proficiency level first or provide the text in the students' preferred language.

Example Scaffold: Alternative Texts

To introduce a novel that the teacher knows is written above some students' proficiency levels, he first provides students with the option of reading portions of the novel in simpler English or in their native language. He then provides short passages of the original text alongside the alternative versions and leads students through comprehension activities in which they demonstrate ultimate comprehension of the original text.

Having the opportunity to understand the meaning of a passage first through easier texts can then assist the learner in building meaning when they tackle the more difficult text.

Outlines

Providing students with outlines prior to listening or reading can help them get an overall sense of what they will be learning. Then, as they listen or read, it can be a helpful reference to help them stay on track.

Example Scaffold: Outlines

Students will be listening to a video-recorded lecture. Prior to the listening task, the teacher provides and outline of the content of the lectures. The teacher talks through the outline, making sure students understand the concepts and words. As students then listen to the lecture, the teacher asks them to put a checkmark beside each line on the outline, as the speaker addresses that topic. As she walks around the room, she can see from students' checkmarks whether they are following along with the lecture.

The outline provides written words to accompany an oral lecture. It also provides the sequence of the topics addressed in the lecture. The activity of checking off the topics as they are addressed keeps students engaged in active listening, and lets the teacher know if students are following along.

Visual supports

Visual supports are essential scaffolds for beginning language learners. It's hard to imagine a language class in which students are learning basic nouns such as food and clothing, without real objects or pictures of those objects. Visuals such as photographs and graphics can provide helpful scaffolding at higher language levels as well. Here are three kinds of visual support:

- ➤ **Realia:** This is the term used for real objects brought into the classroom. In beginning-level language instruction, it can be helpful to bring real food, clothing, kitchen utensils, and other relevant items into the classroom. When students are able to handle real items, there is little chance of misunderstanding what the item is, as can be the case with pictures. Also, it may be easier to remember a word when the item is being handled as the word is being learned.

- ➤ **Pictures:** We often show students pictures as they are learning new words and concepts. These may be drawings or photographs, or even videos. Clear photographs of real objects are usually best, as drawings might not be interpreted correctly if the concept or item is foreign to the student. When using pictures to convey abstract concepts, it is important to remember that different cultures can have very different interpretations of concepts. For example, a teacher might choose a visual of a bird being let out of a cage to represent "freedom." However, in a culture where many people have birds in cages, this visual might not have a positive connotation, and a different visual might better communicate the idea of freedom.

➤ **Graphics:** These include tables, charts, and graphic organizers, and can communicate ideas and relationships. For example, as a student learns the sentence pattern for stating similarities and differences, the teacher might use the visual of a Venn diagram. This Venn diagram (see Figure 4) could be used to support a student's ability to produce this comparative sentence: "A snack and a meal are both food. But a snack is less food and a meal is more food."

See more examples of different kinds of graphics for scaffolding on the companion website for this book (www.tesol.org/ELTBasics).

All of these visuals can be used in multiple ways. We probably most often think of using pictures or realia to show the meanings of new words, but these could also be used to preview a text, or to provide prompts for retelling a text. For example, imagine that a higher level student is tasked with reading a narrative about an event, then retelling that narrative to classmates in a small group. The student would find the task more easily doable if the text had picture prompts to accompany the narrative: Instead of having to return to the text to

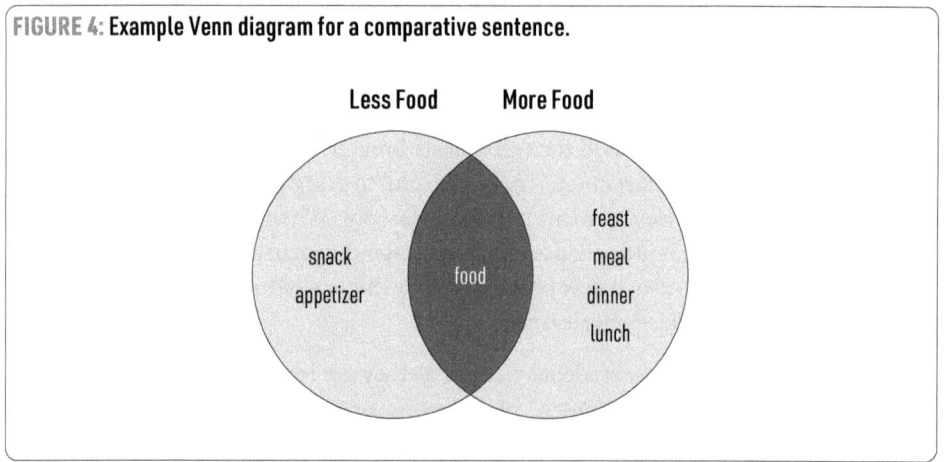

FIGURE 4: **Example Venn diagram for a comparative sentence.**

reread, the student could rely on the pictures to help him remember and share what happened. Table 1 shows some other ways to use visuals with your class:

TABLE 1. Examples of Classroom Use for Selected Visual Scaffolds

Type of Visual	Examples of Classroom Use
Timelines	Teach about tenses, time expressions, daily or weekly schedules, and series/order of events.
Charts and graphs	• Teach superlatives and comparatives. • Support students in selecting adverbs of frequency (e.g., *frequently, rarely*). • Provide visual data for making cause/effect statements. • Teach verbs of change (e.g., *increase/decrease*).
Venn Diagrams	• Support students' use of language to report on similarities and differences.
Realia	• Help beginning students learn the names of objects. • Have students engage in role-plays using the items.
Comic strips	• Have students fill in speech bubbles with their own narratives or stories. • Have students write out a narrative version of the comic strip story. • Delete some of the text in speech bubbles and have students fill it in.

6. Corrective Feedback

An important teacher skill is the ability to help students correct errors and produce accurate language. Here are a few basic best practices for providing corrective feedback:

Best Practices in Providing Corrective Feedback

➤ Be positive. Errors are a normal part of learning a new language. Students should be praised for attempts to use new language, even when they produce errors.

➤ Focus only on errors that are at the student's proficiency level.

- Limit corrections. Don't interrupt students' oral communication to correct every error. Don't correct every error on students' writing—instead, focus on one or two errors that are at the students' level.
- Be sensitive to the student's emotional state. Don't correct when it might cause embarrassment or raise the affective filter.
- Give students opportunities to correct errors.
- Elicit oral reformulations.
- Allow students to resubmit written work.

Correcting spoken language

As previously mentioned, it is not always appropriate to correct spoken language. However, if the teacher determines that the error is at the student's proficiency level, the affective filter is low, and this is the opportune time to help a student improve in accuracy, following are some techniques teachers can use to elicit corrected language.

Emphasis on error

This technique is best when the student is capable of correcting the error. After an error is made, the teacher emphasizes it in some way, such as by

- holding up five fingers, linking each word to a finger, then emphasizing that there is an error in the second word.
- writing the sentence and inserting a blank for the incorrect word or structure, and indicating that something different is needed there.
- repeating the sentence, emphasizing the incorrect word or structure, and ending with question intonation.

Here's an example:

Student: I go to town yesterday.

Teacher: I *go* to town yesterday?

Student: [Student thinks] I *went* to town yesterday.

Teacher: Good!

Meaning reminder

This technique is useful when the student knows the meanings of words and just needs a reminder. Here is an example:

Student: I go to town yesterday.

Teacher: Remember, *yesterday* is in the past.

Student: Oh, yes. I *went* to town yesterday.

Teacher: Good!

Grammar reminder

This technique is used when the student has already learned the grammar, and just needs a reminder. Here is an example:

Student: I go to town yesterday.

Teacher: Remember, *go* is present tense. What is past tense?

Student: Oh, yes. I *went* to town yesterday.

Teacher: Good!

New learning

This technique is effective when the student has not yet learned the word or grammar point:

Student: I go to town yesterday.

Teacher: Yesterday is in the past. Use *went* to talk about the past.

Student: I *went* to town yesterday?

Teacher: Yes, very good! [Teacher leads the student to produce the sentence several times.]

> **Take Note**
> Students are not likely to understand and start to use a correct form or word just from hearing the teacher use it in natural conversation. They need to use the correct form themselves, to begin the process of changing the word or phrase.

A note about recasts

One common way of responding to a student error is called a recast. This is when the teacher follows a student error with a corrected form, but without drawing attention to the error, like in this exchange:

Student: I go to town yesterday.

Teacher: Oh, you went to town yesterday! What did you do in town?

This kind of exchange can be helpful in building students' confidence in their ability to communicate; the student may feel successful because the teacher understood them. Notice, though, that in this exchange, the student does not produce the corrected form, *went*, so it's unlikely that this exchange has helped the student learn that *went* is the past form of *go* and should be used when talking about events in the past. The student has not learned this because the teacher has not elicited a corrected sentence. In other words, the teacher has not helped the student notice and correct the error.

Correcting written language

When correcting student writing, it is important to remember the earlier best practices list, such as limiting the number of corrections and ensuring that they are at the student's proficiency level. When correcting writing, it can be helpful to take a three-stage approach:

- ➤ **Stage 1:** Provide a general indication that there is an error. You might put a checkmark in the margin of a line that contains an error, or highlight a sentence or phrase that contains an error. This provides some direction for the student but also allows an opportunity for self-correction.

- ➤ **Stage 2:** Provide an indication of the type of error. This might be done by writing in an error code above the error. For example, if a student writes "He go to the store yesterday," you might write "VT" for "verb tense" above the word "go." (See the companion website, www.tesol.org/ELTBasics, for a suggested list of error correction codes.)

- ➤ **Stage 3:** Provide the correction. If the student has not been able to produce the corrected form through the feedback in Stages 1 and 2, it may be best to give the student the corrected form. This can be done informally, through conversation with the student about their writing.

This sequence encourages student effort in self-correction while still providing support. After errors have been corrected, it is very helpful for students to rewrite the text, using the corrected language. This helps the corrections to "stick."

To summarize, corrective feedback on both oral and written language is important in ELT. Corrective feedback should be given when errors are at the student's proficiency level, when they do not disrupt communication, and when students are emotionally prepared to learn and grow through corrections. Finally, it is important for the student to produce the corrected language, either in speech or in writing, for the corrected form to begin to take the place of the incorrect form in long-term memory.

7. Teacher Reflection

No chapter on teaching would be complete without mentioning the importance of teachers reflecting on their teaching. As teachers reflect on what worked well and what didn't and what kinds of activities resulted in more and improved language use, they hone their skills in language instruction. In addition, reflecting on student growth, gaps, and needs can help teachers plan future instruction, providing targeted additional practice if needed and slowing down or speeding up the pace in going through the curriculum.

There are countless ways for a teacher to reflect on their teaching; here are a few ways:

- ➤ Take time at the end of each week to journal about what worked well and what didn't.
- ➤ Reflect at the end of each day on students' participation in class, thinking about ways to improve engagement.
- ➤ Use student scores to chart what language is being learned well and what may require more or different types of instruction.

However it is done, reflection on the teaching and learning that occurs in your classroom should become a habit and should influence your planning of future lessons.

Chapter Summary

This chapter has provided some basic concepts about planning and teaching a lesson for MLE language acquisition.

> In ELT contexts focused on learning to speak the language and on using it for communicative purposes, the Aims-Activities-Assessment "Triple A" method of planning can work well.

> Teachers need to gear their teacher talk to the language proficiency levels of the students. In most contexts, teachers need to speak slowly and clearly to facilitate student language acquisition.

> Teachers should group students purposefully for different kinds of interaction and language use.

> Scaffolding is helpful for language development. Teachers can scaffold student language development in various ways, including preteaching, modeling, and using hand gestures for sentence structures.

> Language learners benefit from teachers who provide corrective feedback on errors and who help learners produce corrected language.

> Teachers should reflect on the teaching and learning that takes place in the classroom to improve teaching skills and to target instruction to learners' needs.

CHAPTER 5

Assessment in ELT

Assessment is important in all areas of education, but perhaps more so in English language teaching (ELT) because it can determine admittance and placement of learners in language and academic programs. It can also alert us to any additional challenges they might be facing as we plan their instruction and support. Teachers may have several questions about types and uses of assessments, such as

- how to determine a student's level of proficiency in English,
- what types and methods of assessments are the most effective and least threatening for their students, and
- what a grade in a language classroom should be based upon.

This chapter first discusses terms, purposes, and qualities of language assessments. It then focuses on classroom-based assessment, highlighting three specific and effective methods. This is followed by a discussion on the role of standardized testing in language assessment and then, finally, proficiency levels.

Assessment Terminology

There is sometimes confusion about terms used to talk about assessment. Three common terms that are important to understand are:

- assessment
- evaluation
- testing

Assessment

Assessment is an overarching term that usually simply means collecting or finding evidence of what a student can do. It's often used to mean ongoing assessment. Ongoing, classroom-based assessment can also be called *formative*: **Formative assessment** that is for the purpose of forming, or teaching, the student. Formative assessment is as much for the teacher as for the student. The teacher regularly assesses student learning and uses that knowledge to plan appropriate lessons.

Evaluation

Evaluation is another overarching term. It's often used in connection with judging or interpreting the assessment information that is collected. For example, a teacher may evaluate student output to give a grade. Evaluation is often linked to **summative assessment**, referring to an evaluation at the end of a course of study, rather than ongoing (formative) assessment for the purposes improving teaching and learning. To summarize:

- *Formative assessment* "forms" the teaching and learning throughout the course.
- *Summative evaluation* "sums up" the learning at the end of the course.

Testing

A final word that is used in multiple ways is *testing*. This is sometimes also used interchangeably with *assessment* and *evaluation*. In reality, however, tests are one type of assessment—a type that is frequently used for the purpose of evaluation. Tests are often used for summative purposes.

Standardized testing, the use of official tests to gauge achievement, introduces us to yet another term: *normative*. A norm-referenced test will show how a particular student compares to others.

Assessment Purposes

In ELT, there are three main purposes for assessment:

- placement
- progress
- achievement

When a student begins English language study at a school or with a teacher, one of the first questions the teacher must ask is: What is this student's level of English proficiency? That information will guide what class the student is placed in, what materials will be used, and what accommodations will be needed. This initial testing to determine language level is often called **placement testing**.

The second purpose of assessment, and probably the most common, is determining progress. When a teacher gives a test after a unit of instruction, they intend to discover whether students have made the learning progress expected. Progress assessment can be as simple as an informal checklist that the teacher fills out as students are engaging in classroom tasks. It could also include quizzes, oral questioning, quick-writes, and other ways to elicit from students what they have learned. Progress assessment is often formative in nature: It is to see where students are in their learning and providing direction for future teaching and learning.

Finally, assessments can be used to measure achievement. After a semester in an English class, for example, the school, teacher, and students may want to know how much and what language have been achieved. Final exams, presentations, and essays may all be examples of assessment to determine achievement.

Language Proficiency Level

Whatever the purpose, the goal of language assessment is to understand more about where a multilingual learner of English (MLE) is on their path to becoming a fully competent user of English. In other words, the goal is to learn about the student's language proficiency. So, it's important to understand language proficiency levels and their central role in designing instruction and assessment that will achieve the teaching and learning goals.

Understanding Language Proficiency Levels

There are many ways to describe language learner proficiency levels. Students who are just starting to learn English may be called *beginning*, *elementary*, or *early* learners. When basic words and simple structures have been mastered, students move on to an *intermediate* phase. And when students can communicate fairly well but still need more language work to be fully proficient, we call them *advanced* learners.

At each level, there can still be quite a bit of variation in what learners know and can do. For example, beginning levels can be further divided into a number of designations, such as the following:

- *Raw beginners:* These are students who don't know any English at all.

- *False beginners:* These are students who already know some basic words and phrases (e.g., numbers, the alphabet, and common phrases like "What is your name?" and "How are you?"). False beginners are common in English classes.

- *Literacy students:* This is an MLE who has not learned to read and write in their native language. As this student learns English, they will also be learning basic literacy, which ideally would include literacy in their home language.

At the other end of the spectrum, it's important to realize that even advanced learners, especially those who are adults, often know many fewer words, idioms, and expressions than fluent speakers. An English student may test as advanced, yet only be reading at a Grade 5 level, or an advanced student who is a business professional, for example, might know only 20% of the English words a fluent colleague regularly uses, including specialized vocabulary that isn't taught in regular language programs.

Proficiency Level Scales and Descriptors

There are multiple language proficiency scales. Some of the most internationally recognized include ACTFL, the Common European Framework of Reference (CEFR), and WIDA. Link to more about these and other proficiency scales on the companion website (www.tesol.org/ELTBasics).

In Table 1, the language proficiency chart from *6 Principles for the Exemplary Teaching of English Learners*® provides descriptors of student abilities at each level.

TABLE 1. English Language Development Levels From *The 6 Principles for Exemplary Teaching of English Learners: Grades K–12*®

	Utterance variety and control	Vocabulary use	Communicative functions and registers
Level 1	Relies on memorized phrases	Uses a small vocabulary of high-frequency words	Engages in a few types of familiar exchanges; requires native language or nonverbal supports for academic tasks
Level 2	Produces a variety of memorized phrases and a limited range of sentence patterns	Uses mostly high-frequency words and some content words	Participates in very simple verbal and written interactions; performs academic tasks with native language or other supports
Level 3	Forms a range of phrase and sentence patterns	Uses high and mid-frequency words, plus a few hundred content words	Interacts in most everyday situations, conveys information and asks questions; performs academic tasks with modifications
Level 4	Forms a wider range of utterance patterns with growing accuracy	Uses mid-frequency words as well as hundreds of technical and content words and some idioms	Participates in social interaction; expresses meaning in multiple, related sentences; distinguishes formal and informal registers; performs many academic tasks
Level 5	Forms a variety of utterance patterns into connected discourse with growing accuracy	Uses several thousand technical and content words as well as frequently used idioms and fixed expressions	Participates in extended discourse; switches purposefully between informal and formal registers; performs a wide range of communicative functions and academic tasks
Level 6 (Exited EL status, at grade-level language ability)	Fluently produces grade-level utterance patterns with accuracy	Uses grade-level vocabulary, including a variety of idioms and fixed expressions	Performs grade-level communicative functions, using informal and formal registers appropriately; performs academic tasks independently

EL = English learner
Reproduced with permission from *The 6 Principles for Exemplary Teaching of English Learners: Grades K–12*, by TESOL International Association, 2018, p. 19. Copyright 2018 by TESOL International Association.

Qualities of Assessments

There are many different ways in which assessments can be measured to determine their degree of effectiveness. Four important ways are the following:

- validity
- reliability
- practicality
- washback

Validity

An assessment is considered valid if it measures what it is intended to measure. For example, if a teacher has just taught past tense forms and wants to see if students have learned what she has taught, she may design a simple fill-in-the-blank test asking students to provide the past forms of verbs. This may have **validity** if the teacher wants to assess this passive knowledge. However, what if this teacher actually wants students be able to use past tense forms in real communication? If this is the teacher's (and students') goal, then the fill-in-the-blank test is not the most valid assessment because it doesn't measure students' real use of past tense forms.

Reliability

Reliability has to do with the degree to which we can depend on the results of an assessment. That is, will the test produce the same results every time? For example, it is important that a standardized test providing a language proficiency score be reliable. If a student takes the test multiple times only several days apart, the score should be roughly the same each time. Reliability is a very important factor in high-stakes testing, but much less so in ongoing, formative classroom assessment.

Practicality

Practicality is a word that may not be often thought of in relation to assessment. Language assessments vary in how practical they are to administer, and given that all educational systems have time and financial constraints, practicality is an important consideration. Practicality must be considered in conjunction with the purposes of assessment. When assessing students for placement, schools and teachers need assessments that are quick, efficient, and cost effective. A simple multiple-choice test, for example, in conjunction with a short oral interview, might provide a rough idea of a student's proficiency level, and this might be sufficient for placing the student in the correct class, or with the right materials. A high-stakes achievement test, however, must be valid and reliable; creators of such tests often spend quite a bit of money piloting such tests to ensure that they are.

Washback

A final important quality of language assessments is **washback**: the effect of assessment on instruction. Washback can be either positive or negative. If the assessment system is such that it promotes the achievement of the learning goals, then washback is positive.

For example, imagine that a goal for beginners in an English as a second language class is to be able to ask school personnel about how to get to various places in the school. If students are assessed on this ability at the end of the course with a classroom simulation of a dialogue with the school secretary, for example, the washback would be positive. Students would be accomplishing the learning objective as they prepare for the assessment.

Washback is frequently negative, however. Imagine the same learner classroom with the same end goal, but the assessment at the end of the course is a written test emphasizing grammar, spelling, and vocabulary forms. Because the students and teacher know they need to prepare for this test, precious class time is spent on grammar, spelling, and vocabulary—not on developing the communication skills to interact with school personnel. The goals are not met in this case precisely because of the negative washback of the final test.

Classroom-Based Assessment

Classroom-based, formative assessment is the most helpful kind of assessment in language acquisition. Informal assessment that is integrated into the learning activities should be a part of every lesson, as addressed in Chapter 4. A simple chart like the one shown in Figure 1 can be a useful tool for this kind of assessment, and it can be used for any type of skill development.

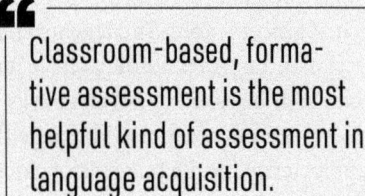

> Classroom-based, formative assessment is the most helpful kind of assessment in language acquisition.

In addition, teachers usually must design assessments to determine overall learning and, often, to assign a grade. For such assessments,

FIGURE 1: Informal language acquisition checklist.

		Student has significant difficulty	Student has some difficulty	Student shows mastery
Date	Student			

Linguistic item being assessed: _____

it can be helpful to understand three ways of designing classroom-based language assessments:

- using performance tasks
- involving students in their own assessment
- creating portfolios

Performance Tasks

Performance, in the field of second language acquisition, simply means that students will use language, and that teachers will assess how well they perform as they read, write, speak, or listen in English. It does not mean that students are presenting in front of the class, or "performing" for others. A task in ELT is something students are asked to do with the language. For example, a language task might be to engage in dialogue needed to purchase items in a grocery store. The teacher might simulate this kind of real-world task in the language classroom. After students have had opportunities to acquire language through tasks, they can then be asked to perform very similar tasks for assessment purposes. Any activity that requires students to use language that they have learned, demonstrating communicative competence for the purpose of assessment, is a performance task.

The advantages of performance tasks over more traditional types of assessments, such as pen and paper tests, are obvious: students are assessed on real communicative ability rather than on passive language knowledge. Performance tasks can be relatively simple, such as assessing students' ability to introduce themselves by stating their name, where they live, and what they do or study. Alternatively, this fairly simple task could be one in a series of small tasks leading to a larger performance task, such as engaging in a simulated job interview.

Performance tasks are often evaluated using **rubrics**. A rubric defines what constitutes acceptable task performance and shows students if and how their performance could be improved. Figure 2 shows a possible rubric for the aforementioned performance task: engaging in a simulated job interview. After students have learned pertinent language and information about job interviews and after they have had opportunities to engage in at least one simulated job interview as practice, the teacher could then set up an interview as a performance task for the purpose of assessment. As the student engages in the task, the teacher evaluates the performance in each of the four categories shown on the left. Each receives the number of points in accordance with performance, as shown across the top, for a total of 10 possible points.

Rubrics are sometimes classified as either analytic or holistic. An analytic rubric typically assesses a completed product or performance task, such as the rubric shown in Figure 2. A holistic rubric assesses student work as a whole, over time. For example, a holistic rubric might be used to assess a group project, including participation in various group meetings, peer evaluations, and contributions to the final product.

Creating a rubric can seem daunting at first. These tips may help.

1. Make sure that criteria in the rubric relate to the course objectives.

2. Consider which specific areas of knowledge and skill you want students to demonstrate through the task.

3. Select an appropriate number of criteria for the complexity of the task, and the weight it carries for the students' grades. A shorter, simpler task might have three to four criteria, while a more complex and more important final performance task might have six to seven.

4. Consider how criteria will be observed and measured. Will you be able to adequately observe and evaluate a criterion as students are engaged in performance? Or will you need to record a performance task and watch it later, when you can stop to take notes?

See additional examples of rubrics on the companion website at www.tesol.org/ELTBasics.

FIGURE 2. Example rubric for a performance task: engaging in a simulated job interview.

	Points: 0.0–0.9	Points: 1.0–1.4	Points: 1.5–1.9	Points: 2.0–2.5
Introduction and qualifications for job ___ / 2.5	Student needs to improve in all of these areas: ☐ Gives name and other pertinent personal information ☐ Tells about pertinent education ☐ Tells about pertinent experience	Student needs to improve in two of these areas: ☐ Gives name and other pertinent personal information ☐ Tells about pertinent education ☐ Tells about pertinent experience	Student needs to improve in one of these areas: ☐ Gives name and other pertinent personal information ☐ Tells about pertinent education ☐ Tells about pertinent experience	Student excels in all areas: ☐ Gives name and other pertinent personal information ☐ Tells about pertinent education ☐ Tells about pertinent experience
Cultural appropriateness ___ / 2.5	Student needs to improve in all of these areas: ☐ Friendly and positive ☐ Dressed appropriately ☐ Asks questions and shows interest ☐ Uses appropriate forms of address ☐ Is neither boastful nor reticent	Student needs to improve in three or four of these areas: ☐ Friendly and positive ☐ Dressed appropriately ☐ Asks questions and shows interest ☐ Uses appropriate forms of address ☐ Is neither boastful nor reticent	Student needs to improve in one or two of these areas: ☐ Friendly and positive ☐ Dressed appropriately ☐ Asks questions and shows interest ☐ Uses appropriate forms of address ☐ Is neither boastful nor reticent	Student excels in all areas: ☐ Friendly and positive ☐ Dressed appropriately ☐ Asks questions and shows interest ☐ Uses appropriate forms of address ☐ Is neither boastful nor reticent

	Points: 0.0–0.9	Points: 1.0–1.4	Points: 1.5–1.9	Points: 2.0–2.5
Answering questions ___ / 2.5	Needs to improve in all of these areas: ☐ Answers questions promptly ☐ Uses "stall" techniques as appropriate ☐ Uses mostly positive responses	Needs to improve in two of these areas: ☐ Answers questions promptly ☐ Uses "stall" techniques as appropriate ☐ Uses mostly positive responses	Needs to improve in one of these areas: ☐ Answers questions promptly ☐ Uses "stall" techniques as appropriate ☐ Uses mostly positive responses	Student excels in all areas: ☐ Answers questions promptly ☐ Uses "stall" techniques as appropriate ☐ Uses mostly positive responses
Language, including: • Grammatical forms • Word choice • Sentence complexity • Pronunciation and intonation ___ / 2.5	Student has many errors in language use. Errors often interfere with communication.	Student has frequent errors in language use. Errors sometimes interfere with communication.	Student's use of language is good, with occasional minor errors. Errors do not interfere with communication.	Student's use of language is excellent, with very few errors. Errors do not interfere with communication.

Score _____

Because rubrics bring clarity to what is expected in performance and specificity in how students can improve, they should be utilized at the beginning of a learning task or assignment. Going over the rubric when an assignment is introduced can help learners know what is expected and help teachers align instruction to assessment. At the conclusion of the task, using the rubric for grading can help learners understand how they can improve.

Student Involvement in Assessment

The teacher's role in the language classroom is to provide experiences that can result in language acquisition. However, fully engaging in these experiences is the responsibility of the learner. Involving students in assessing their progress can help them realize this responsibility and invest in the opportunities provided for them. Students should be able to identify signs of learning, note weaknesses and areas for improvement, and set their own learning goals. There are many tools that teachers can utilize to help students do this.

Learning logs are notebooks in which students record their daily learning, or charts provided by the teacher to note learning activities, degree of success, and further goals. Learning logs can be a useful part of a self-evaluation scheme in which learners formally assess their learning periodically in the course. Self-assessment can even contribute to the grading scheme.

Journals can also be utilized in a multitude of ways to involve students in assessment. They may be an expanded form of learning log, written in narrative rather than note form, thus improving writing skills as well. Journals can be shared between teacher and learner; these shared journals are sometimes called *dialogue journals*. This type of journal involves students in assessment as teachers pose questions, such as "What did you learn today?" or "What can you do to improve your pronunciation?" They can also be a form of ongoing conversation between teacher and student.

Reflections are another common writing task used for involving students in their own assessment. Students can reflect on interactions in English outside the class, their feelings about the language acquisition process, their speculations on activities they could engage in to make faster progress—any number of reflective issues or topics relating to assessment could be addressed. Reflection is often thought of as a written task, but it can occur orally as well.

Portfolios

A final tool for classroom-based assessment is the portfolio. A portfolio is a collection of items, sometimes called artifacts, that demonstrate language acquisition. Portfolios may be designed for two purposes:

- *Demonstrating progress:* These portfolios show work at various stages to highlight the progress that has been made.
- *Demonstrating achievement:* These portfolios don't show progress over time, but rather focus on the student's current ability.

Whatever the focus and goal, portfolios provide students with an opportunity to show how they can use their new language. Artifacts of student writing have in the past been the easiest to include in portfolios. However, with the option of online portfolios, audio and visual files demonstrating oral skills are just as easy to include. Other artifacts could be visual representations of learning, such as a chart showing new words learned, or a graphic comparing the home language and English. Students could also include visuals that represent successful communication, such as a photograph of them with a store clerk, accompanied by a brief written description of the interaction.

Portfolios are usually most successful in documenting performance and engaging students in assessment when specific guidelines are in place. For example, these guidelines might be appropriate:

Portfolio Guidelines

1. There is a limited number of artifacts (usually under 10), and they meet specific guidelines correlating to the learning goals.
2. Students must include an introduction to the portfolio as well as an explanation of each artifact.
3. Students must include a summary reflection on their learning.
4. The portfolio must be attractive and inviting.

* * *

All of these types of classroom-based assessment can go together. For example, a teacher might design lessons on responding to questions and might utilize the informal checklist in Figure 1 in these lessons. The lessons might culminate in the simulated interview performance task earlier in the chapter, utilizing the rubric in Figure 2. The teacher might video the interview, and the student might watch it later, filling out a self-assessment. Finally, the rubric, video, and self-assessment might be added to the student's portfolio as evidence of language growth.

Cultural Factors

No discussion of assessment in language acquisition would be complete without addressing the issue of culture.

Cultural Expectations

Students will have preexisting perspectives about assessment, evaluation, and testing that come from their cultural backgrounds. For example, they might believe that pen and paper tests are the only valid form of measurement or that students cannot possibly participate in their own assessment. Such cultural perspectives are important to consider. Rather than dismissing student opinions when they clash with what we consider to be good language assessment, we can engage in respectful dialogue and possibly find a middle ground in using both assessments that students feel are valid and some alternative types of assessment, such as portfolios and self-assessment.

Students are not the only ones bringing cultural expectations to the issue of assessment. Standardized testing is the main form of assessment in many schools. As a result, some teachers and school leaders may view these types of tests as the most credible form of assessment. As you try some different types of assessments, you may have opportunities to expand the view of what qualifies for effective assessment in your context.

Cultural Competence

Another cultural issue in testing is the content of the tests—especially on standardized tests. Cultural background can significantly impact students' understanding of words and situations. Consider the scenario of a student who has emigrated from Jakarta, Indonesia, to the United States. In Jakarta, the student lived in an apartment complex, as did virtually everyone he knew. The houses he has seen have been surrounded by walls. The student reads this question on a standardized test:

Which of these items would NOT be in a yard:

a. A barbecue

b. A TV

c. Grass

d. A dog

First, the student may never have seen an American-style yard. Second, the student may envision dogs as dirty pests which roam the city. He may be aware that some people keep them as pets, but may reason that, if this is the case, the dog would be kept inside. Finally, he may picture the outdoor entertainment area of his apartment complex in Jakarta, which includes a TV. So, he may come to the conclusion that *d* is the correct response. This question likely was designed to show whether or not the student knew the meaning of the word *yard*. The student did have an understanding of *yard* as an outdoor living space, but lacked the cultural background to select the correct choice to demonstrate his understanding.

It is critically important that language tests measure language—not cultural knowledge.

Even internationally used tests may have readings or questions which students in some contexts do not have the cultural background to interpret. For this reason, it is important to include multiple sources of information for high-stakes assessment, such as admission to university programs. When a standardized test is accompanied by an interview and a written essay, for example, the multiple data points can help to correct a low test score due to lack of cultural background.

Standardized Testing

In many places, standardized testing is regularly used for placement, progress, and achievement. It is beyond the scope of this book to discuss mandated tests, procedures, and policies in detail, as those vary from context to context. Though there are legitimate reasons for standardized tests, such as placement in programs and collecting data on overall student achievement, there are also some pitfalls of standardized testing:

➤ Standardized test scores may not accurately reflect students' linguistic abilities. For example, a written test doesn't show a student's oral competence, and a test focusing on explicit grammar knowledge may not show that a student can use grammar forms correctly but simply doesn't know what they are called.

➤ Preparation for standardized testing may divert classroom time from activities that would help students develop communicative competence. As more classroom time is spent on test preparation, less is available to help students actually acquire the language for real communication. As mentioned earlier in this chapter, we call this negative washback.

➤ Standardized testing may be a significant source of stress for students. We know that stress inhibits language acquisition. Standardized testing, especially if it's "high-stakes," with significant ramifications for students' work and study goals, can work against the language acquisition process.

Teachers usually have little say over standardized testing. However, knowledge of these challenges can help teachers to mitigate the possible negative effects and can help them increase students' understanding of goals and testing. In addition, sometimes teachers can advocate for changes in standardized testing practices. (See the companion website for this book for examples of how teachers can become testing advocates: www.tesol.org/ELTBasics.)

Chapter Summary

English language teaching contexts are very diverse, with assessment systems and realities that vary considerably from setting to setting. Who controls assessment and the purpose for which it is used can range from complete teacher and student control to mandated government assessments, which are rigid in both timing and content. All stakeholders can benefit from understanding the following about assessment:

> Assessment is helpful in language acquisition when it accurately reflects the degree to which a student has reached the learning aims or objectives.

> Formative, in-class assessment should be routinely used by classroom teachers, both to guide future instruction and to help students focus their learning.

> Assessments need to measure what they claim to measure. (E.g., only an oral test can measure speaking ability.)

> Assessments are not limited to tests. Portfolios, self-evaluations, and performance tasks can all contribute to language assessment.

> Rubrics can be helpful for both teachers and students in preparing for and evaluating performance tasks.

> In contexts where assessment systems are mandated, purposeful steps can be taken to limit the possible negative washback that testing could have on language instruction and to enable students to still achieve their language goals.

Using assessment to its full potential within ELT classrooms can help teachers and students work together to ensure that student goals are met.

CHAPTER 6

ELT Skills and Activities

Chapter 4 introduced English language teaching (ELT) lesson planning in which activities play a starring role. Many activities done in ELT classrooms simply consist of pairs or groups of students interacting to complete a task or to communicate on specific topics. At other times, though, it can be helpful to have some activity templates to draw from to create lessons that are diverse and engaging. This chapter introduces several such activity templates. Many of these can be used not only for instruction, but also for ongoing, formative assessment.

This chapter also provides an introduction to language skills and the different ways in which we practice them. The language skills, also sometimes called modalities, are listening, speaking, reading, and writing (with grammar and pronunciation considered as auxiliary skills). These skills overlap in several different ways because they commonly develop concurrently, and they are often referred to in these overlapping pairs:[2]

Overlapping Skills		Term
Listening and speaking	>	Oracy
Reading and writing	>	Literacy

This chapter addresses three broad types of activities:

- ➤ Those that develop listening and speaking skills
- ➤ Those that develop reading and writing skills
- ➤ Those that can integrate all four skill areas

---

2. Listening and reading (receptive skills) are sometimes paired, as are speaking and writing (productive skills); some people have developed receptive skills while not developing production, and vice versa.

Each section begins with an introduction to the skill areas, including tips for teaching. It then introduces a series of activities to practice those skills.

Some of the activities showcased here have accompanying sample worksheets in Appendix B, available in downloadable form on the companion website for this book (www.tesol.org/ELTBasics). Each activity gives the proficiency levels that it is suitable for, a short description, steps for conducting the activity, and possible variations. Most activities can have many more variations than those listed. It may be helpful to engage in the activities as they are written the first few times before making changes for different types of practice.

For all activities, regardless of which skill is being developed, ensure that the activities are at students' proficiency level.

All of the activities in this book are intended to use language at your students' proficiency level. Also note that though the activities in this chapter often provide general examples and topics, you should personalize the content and language used so that it's relevant to students' contexts.

Speaking and Listening

Language students need many opportunities to hear and comprehend the new language, and to begin to produce it for meaningful communication. Following are some tips for helping multilingual learners of English (MLEs) develop oral skills.

Tips

1. Ensure that students know what they should do in a speaking activity.

2. Use activities that require students to look at their listeners as they speak rather than having their eyes on a text.

3. As much as possible, use oral activities that simulate real-world dialogue and interactions.

4. When possible, provide input using real people. It is much easier to comprehend a real person speaking than listening to a recorded voice or dialogue.

5. Give students time to produce oral language. Resist the temptation to jump in and help students too quickly.

6. A beginning student may be in a silent period. Allow them time to be silent. Allow them to respond through actions rather than with words.

7. Use more pair than small or large group activities to encourage speaking aloud; it's often easier to take a speaking risk in a pair than a group.

8. Expect students to produce language at their proficiency level, not above.

Because students may be more fearful of speaking and listening tasks that they are of reading and writing tasks, ensure that activities are at the appropriate level. This will help students more readily engage in the tasks and develop confidence to speak English more often. Following are some helpful scaffolds for listening and speaking activities:

Helpful Scaffolds for Listening and Speaking Activities

- For English learners with early proficiency, it can be helpful to give the instructions in the home or preferred language.

- Model what students need to do.

- Provide prompts, visuals, and written words to support learners so they don't have to remember all the needed vocabulary as they are speaking.

- Introduce prompts before beginning the activity and allow students to write out or think about their responses before splitting into groups or partners.

- For question and answer tasks, provide learners with sample questions and answers on any worksheets they are filling out for the activity.

Listening and Speaking Activities

Group Up

Proficiency Levels: All

This ice-breaker activity can be used to help students mingle or form smaller groups.

Steps

1. Think of some open-ended relational questions, such as "What is your favorite color?" or "What toppings do you like on pizza?"
2. Call out the question and have students "group up" with others who share similar answers.
3. Ask each group to share their answers.

Variations & Tips

- Classes with higher level students can have more complex questions, such as "What is your opinion about solar farms?"

Total Physical Response/TPR (Asher, 1969)

Proficiency Levels: Beginner

In this activity, the teacher gives commands, and the students perform the actions. Beginning students can demonstrate their comprehension without having to speak.

Steps

1. Think of commands that will enable students to learn new words or demonstrate their comprehension of a sentence. For example, "Touch your nose" to teach the word *nose* during a lesson on body parts.
2. Do the action as you speak and motion for students to do it as well.
3. After two or three commands (e.g., *nose, ear, mouth*), begin repeating the commands without doing the action yourself.

4. Gradually introduce more new words, continuing to use all the words in differing order.

Variations & Tips

- Use this activity to help students comprehend sentences instead of single words. For example, "First, close the door, then turn off the light, and finally close the window" to help students learn sequence words.

- Students can take the place of the teacher, calling out commands.

TPR Storytelling (Ray, 1990)

Proficiency Levels: All

This activity is similar to TPR. However, students' actions are in response to a story rather than individual comments. At lower proficiency levels, they may simply listen for specific words or phrases and do actions when they hear them. At higher levels, they may take on roles of characters in the story and act out the story as it is being read.

Steps

1. Select a story text that is at students' language level.

2. Decide how students will provide physical responses, whether by listening for certain words or phrases, or acting out elements of the story.

3. Preteach words, phrases, and actions as needed. If students will be taking on the role of a character in the story, prepare students for listening to the story and acting out what they hear.

4. Read the story aloud. Students respond with actions as they listen.

Variations & Tips

- Have one or more students read the text while the other students respond through actions.

- Have students work in groups to video-record their enactment of the story.

Chants

Proficiency Levels: Beginning

Students participate in chants, gaining in fluency through repetition and attention to intonation and rhythm.

Steps

1. Select or create a chant. (Many English language learning chants can be found with an internet search.) Here is an example of a chant:

    A: Hello, how are you?   B: I'm fine! How are you?

    A: I'm fine. How's Bill?   B: He's fine. How's Mary?

    A: She's fine. How's your cat? B: She's sick!

    A: Oh no!

2. Have someone model the chant with you, so you can show students how it goes.
3. Divide the class into two groups. Assign one group as Speaker A and one as Speaker B. Have them do the chant, then switch roles.

Variations & Tips

- Use chants with more advanced students if the language reflects language they are learning.
- Chants can be fun ways to begin or end the class, or to take a break in the middle.

Surveys

Proficiency Levels: Beginning

Students ask questions of their classmates and fill in a survey showing the responses.

Steps

1. Identify one or more questions that students can ask their classmates. For example, "Do you like ____ (chicken, rain, cats, etc.)?"

2. Create a survey grid (see example in Appendix B) where students can log their classmates' responses.

3. Provide students with the survey grid. Have them mingle with classmates, asking and answering the questions while filling out the survey.

Variations & Tips

➤ More advanced students can ask and answer more complex questions, such as "Who is your favorite superhero, and why?"

➤ More advanced students can create the grid themselves.

Find Someone Who

Proficiency Levels: All

Students ask questions of classmates to find individuals who fit specific criteria.

Steps

1. Create a worksheet with a listing of categories (see example in Appendix B). For MLEs with early proficiency, be sure to write the prompt (what students need to ask others) on the worksheet.

2. Distribute the worksheet. Have students circulate, ask their classmates if they can answer *yes* to any of the questions, and collect signatures.

Variations & Tips

- Use this activity to help students learn about their city or school campus at the beginning of the school year. (E.g., Have you eaten at the student center? Have you been to Castle Bridge?)

- Adapt this activity as a review of any learned material. Simply change the prompt to "Find someone who knows…", and create statements of information that students should have learned.

Upset the Fruit Basket

Proficiency Levels: All

In this game, one student in the middle of a circle tries to get a seat in the circle when students have to change seats. The prompt to change seats can use language that students need to practice.

Steps

1. Think of a language form that students can practice in the form of repetitive but slightly different sentences. The response prompts students to change seats. For example:

    a. Beginning proficiency: "Move if you have a brother" or "Move if you have a pet."

    b. More advanced: "I haven't ever _____. Move if you *have*." And then switch it to:

    "I have _____. Move if you *haven't*."

2. Seat students in a circle, with no empty chairs. You begin in the middle.

3. Give the prompt. For example, "Move if you have a brother." All those who have brothers must switch seats. You try to get one of the empty seats before they are all taken.

4. Whoever is left standing in the middle, without a seat, gives the next prompt.

Variations & Tips

➤ This game can be played standing instead of seated in chairs. Mark spots on the ground or floor using available items, ensuring that there is one less spot than there are students.

➤ It may be helpful to have the sentence frame or prompt available on the board, or on cards that learners can keep with them.

Circle Practice

Proficiency Levels: Beginning

Students in a circle pass objects or pictures around the circle, identifying each one.

Steps

1. Sit with students in a circle. Begin by speaking a word, phrase, or question to a student next to you. That student repeats it to the next student, and so on.

2. Often, simple but complete sentences can be practiced, such as the following:

    Teacher to Student 1: What's this? [handing the student an apple]

    Student 1 to Teacher: It's an apple.

    Student 1 to Student 2: What's this? [handing the student the apple]

    Student 2 to Student 1: It's an apple.

    Student 2 to Student 3: What's this? [handing the student the apple]

    And so on.

3. The apple continues around the circle.

Variations & Tips

➤ If this activity is being used for review rather than for introducing new content, you may start a second phrase after the first has been done by one or two students. For more fun, start another phrase going in the opposite direction around the circle.

➤ Adapt this activity to specific themes and topics. For example, the objects being passed around the circle could all be objects found in a first aid kit.

Circle Memory

Proficiency Levels: All

In this game, students in a circle try to remember and repeat what each previous person has said before adding their own information.

Steps

1. Sit in a circle with students. Begin by introducing a key phrase and your own response. For example, you might say, "I'm going on vacation and I'm going to take an umbrella."

2. The next person must repeat the prompt and what you have said, and they must add something new. For example, the student might say, "I'm going on vacation and I'm going to take an umbrella and a suitcase." The next person must repeat the sentence, adding a new item.

3. Continue going around the circle. The last person will need to remember what each person has named.

Variations & Tips

- If you want students to use specific words, you can give them words or pictures on cards rather than letting them choose their own items.

- The prompt can be designed to practice specific types of grammar. For example, to practice modals, students might be creating sentences such as "If you're sick, you should see a doctor." The following sentences might be, "If you're sick, you should see a doctor and stay in bed," and then "If you're sick, you should see a doctor, stay in bed, and drink lots of water."

Information Gap

Proficiency Levels: All

In this pair activity, students must provide each other with information that they are given in order to complete a task.

Steps

1. Design a task in which students must share information in order to succeed in the task. For example, students might need to fill in the dates of upcoming school events on a calendar. Each student might have half of the information and need to share their information with their partner.

2. Place students in pairs and give them the task. Be sure students know that they need to ask and answer questions to complete the task, not just look at each other's information sheet.

Variations

- Try this activity in a small group if the task warrants several different perspectives. For example, in a task to create a homework policy for a school, students might be in groups of four. Each student would have a card identifying their position on the topic.

- One person in a pair can be given a visual to be replicated. That student tries to describe the visual as their partner re-creates it.

Language Tic-Tac-Toe

Proficiency Levels: Beginning

In this group activity, students must create sentences to place an X or an O on a tic-tac-toe grid.

Steps

1. Create a tic-tac-toe grid, placing words or grammar directives on the left and upper sides. In the example shown here, the words on top are pronouns, and on the side they are verbs:

	he	we	I
go			
take			
like			

2. Divide the class into two teams. Teams take turns requesting an X or an O in a specific square by creating a correct sentence using the words in that square's column or row. For example, if a team wants the middle square in the example grid, they must make a sentence combining "we" and "take," such as "We take the bus to school." If a team wants the top right square, they must make a sentence combining "I" and "go," such as "I go to school every day."

Variations & Tips

- Use this activity to practice many different kinds of words and grammar. For example, the grid in the following example could help students practice singular, plural and uncountable nouns.

	apples	banana	milk
have			
eat			
like			

- Adapt for higher levels using verbs (e.g., *imagine*, *design*, and *create*) and advanced verb tenses (e.g., present perfect, future perfect, and past perfect). Students would need to create sentences using the these verb tenses and verbs.

Bingo

Proficiency Levels: Beginning

In this activity, students hear words and check them off on a Bingo grid. When they get five checked off in a row, they yell out "Bingo!"

Steps

1. Give students a printed Bingo grid of 25 squares, or have them fold a piece of paper to make 16 squares. Direct them to put something specific in each square. For example, to practice number words, you might put 25 or 16 numbers on the board and instruct students to put these randomly on the Bingo grid.

2. Call out the numbers randomly, or have a student call them out, and have students put an X or place a chip over the number they hear.

3. The first student to have a row filled in calls out "Bingo!" Play can end there, or play can continue until all numbers have been called out.

Variations & Tips

➤ There are many variations for practicing different types of words. Here are a few:

> *Practice body part words:* Write body part words on the board for students to copy onto their Bingo grids. Point to a part of your own body, without saying the word. Students must find that word and put an X on it.

> *Practice color words:* Have students color the squares different colors. Call out colors and have students X them out.

> *Practice clothing words:* Bring in many different types of clothing. Put these words on the board and have students write them randomly on their Bingo grids. Pick up a piece of clothing, without saying the word. Students must check off that word on their Bingo grid.

> *Use small pictures of current vocabulary:* These can be cut out and placed randomly on Bingo grids. Instead of putting an X over a square, the picture can simply be removed when the word is called. That way it can be played with the same pictures again and again.

> *Grammar:* Write different verb tenses on the board. Once students have filled in their grids, speak sentences using different tenses. Students must recognize which tense you've used and mark it off on their grid.

Reading and Writing

The purposes of written text vary tremendously, and students might have very different goals for learning to read and write in English. For example, one student might want to just be able to use text on social media, and another might need to read academic texts and write formal essays. These differences become more significant as proficiency increases. In other words, two beginning students can benefit from the same reading and writing tasks, but two intermediate students might need very different reading passages and writing activities. Nevertheless, there are some general tips that apply to the teaching of reading and writing in many contexts.

Tips

1. Ensure that students know what they should do in a reading or writing activity. Provide written instructions.

2. When having students read texts, ensure that they do something with the text. This could be underlining, finding certain types of words, or answering comprehension questions.

3. As much as possible, readings should be drawn from students' interests, and writing tasks should simulate real-world uses of writing.

4. Give students time to think about what they are going to write. Many students need time to warm up to a topic and begin thinking about it.

5. It is not necessary to correct all errors when giving writing feedback. Writing fluency develops more quickly when students feel comfortable taking risks.

6. Have multiple people read a written piece that a student has worked hard on. Posting work on classroom walls or online, if allowed, can provide an audience that makes writing worthwhile.

7. Consider the legibility of words and paragraphs on the page. Consider whether the font type and size, layout, background colors, and so on are optimal for reading ease.

8. If the number of new words in a reading passage make up more than 5% of the reading, the passage may be too difficult. An online readability checker can be helpful in determining reading level. (See one readability checker here: readabilityformulas.com/free-readability-formula-tests.php)

Students may love or hate reading and writing, but some of these feelings might come from past experiences, not from true preferences. When we ensure that texts are at the right level for our MLEs, that they are interesting to students, and that the writing focus will be useful in the real world, we help even reluctant readers and writers to engage more effectively in these skills. Following are some helpful scaffolds for reading and writing activities:

> **Take Note**
>
> **Helpful Scaffolds for Reading and Writing Activities**
>
> - Explain reading and writing tasks *orally*, in English. If needed, also provide students at early proficiency levels with oral instructions in the home or preferred language.
>
> - Activate background knowledge and experiences through discussion prior to reading and writing tasks.
>
> - Preteach key vocabulary prior to a reading task.
>
> - Provide students with reading goals prior to beginning a reading task. For example: "Read this passage to find out three ways to prepare for a job interview."
>
> - Provide a completed model (a mentor text) showing the kind of written text students are expected to produce.
>
> - Provide word sets and sentence frames when asking students to produce writing.

Reading and Writing Activities

Scrambled Sentences

Proficiency Levels: All

In this pair or group game, students put words in order to form sentences.

Steps

1. Create sentences that utilize grammar or vocabulary that students are learning. For each sentence, write each word on a separate card or piece of paper, and place all the words for each sentence in an envelope. Number each envelope, so students can keep track of which ones they have done. On each envelope, also write how many words there should be inside. This ensures that students will know if any words are missing. Have a few more sentences/envelopes than there will be groups or pairs.

2. Place students in small groups (for larger classes) or pairs (for smaller classes).

3. Place all the sentence envelopes on a table or desk at the front of the room. Have one person from each group come up and take an envelope back to their group. The group works together to put the words in order to make a sentence.

4. When they have the words in order, they call you over to check the sentence. If the sentence is correct, they take note on a sheet of paper, put all the words back in the envelope and take it back to the front, and get another one. They should keep track of which ones they have done.

5. The first group to do all the sentences is the winner.

Variations & Tips

➤ You may want to require that each member of the group write down each completed sentence.

➤ If a group or pair is having a lot of difficulty, assist them by providing the first couple of words in the sentence.

➤ Adapt this activity by creating short paragraphs that utilize grammar, vocabulary or discourse features that they are learning and cut up full sentences for each envelope. If a group or pair is having a lot of difficulty, assist them by providing the first and last sentence of the paragraph.

Four-Corners Vocab[3]

Proficiency Levels: All

This is a method of preteaching vocabulary words that might be new in a reading.

Steps

1. Have students work in pairs or small groups.
2. Provide the "Four Corners" template or have students re-create the template on their own paper:

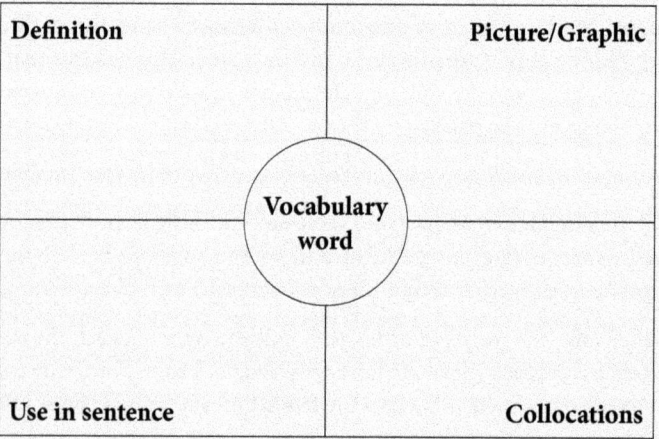

3. Provide the vocabulary word for preteaching, which students will write in the middle.

---

3. The graphic organizer this activity is based on stems from the Frayer Model.

4. Have students work with their partners or groups to fill out all four corners.

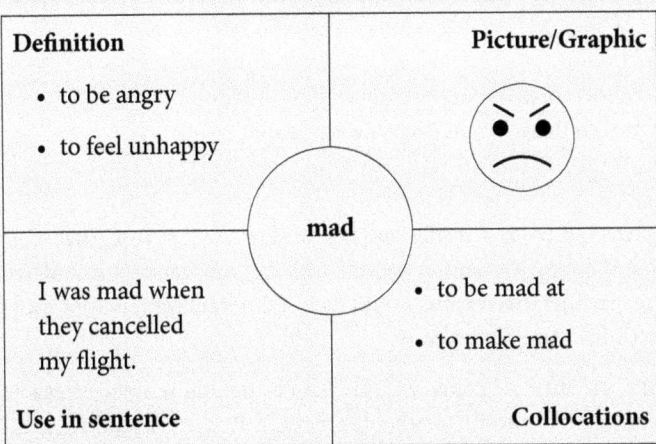

Variations & Tips

➤ For MLEs with early proficiency, "collocations" could be changed to "translation" (providing the word in their home or preferred language).

➤ If a word has several synonyms or related words, the four corners can be used for those. For example:

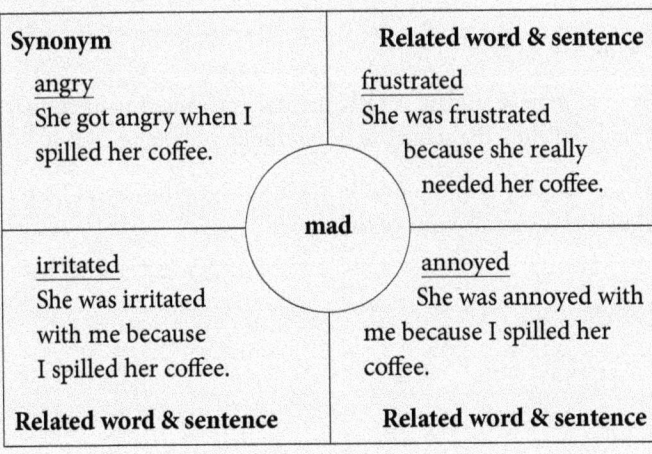

Chain Stories

Proficiency Levels: All

In this activity, sheets of paper are passed around the room. Each student takes a turn adding a sentence to the story on each sheet of paper.

Steps

1. Create sheets of paper (ideally one per student) with a story-starting sentence written at the top. The sentences may utilize grammar or vocabulary that students are learning. Each paper could have a different sentence, or they could all begin with the same sentence.

2. Hand out one sheet of paper with the story-starting sentence to each student. After reading the introductory sentence, each student should write their name at the top, then write a sentence continuing the story. They then fold the paper so the top sentence is no longer visible, and hand the paper to the next student.

3. Each student fills in a subsequent sentence in the story, leaving only their sentence visible when they pass the paper on to the next student.

4. When the papers return to their original owners, students unfold the sheets and read the stories. The stories are often funny and can be read aloud to the whole class.

Variations & Tips

➤ You may want to have students create the starting sentences after giving them a prompt that will elicit the structure or vocabulary being practiced.

➤ Students can correct errors found in their stories. This could be followed by whole class discussion of some of the errors.

Cloze Passages

Proficiency Levels: All

This is normally an individual activity in which students fill in words in a passage.

Steps

1. Select a passage. Delete some words in the passage. There are two methods of doing this:
   a. Delete every fifth to seventh word, ensuring that the word deleted is not a content word that is needed to understand the passage.
   b. Delete all or most of a certain type of word, such as articles, pronouns, or connecting words.
2. Have students read the passage once through, to get the gist.
3. Have them go back through to fill in missing words.
4. In assessing a cloze exercise, normally any acceptable word is admissible, even if it is not the exact word in the original passage.

Variations & Tips

- Have students compare answers and work together to arrive at a more correct passage.
- Have students use the resulting passage as a mentor text to write a paragraph on a similar topic.
- Students can work in pairs. Each reads the same text, and then creates a cloze passage from it. They exchange passages, filling in the blanks.

Air Writing

Proficiency Levels: Beginning

In this activity, students work in pairs or small groups taking turns writing letters in the air as other students guess the letters.

Steps

1. Place students in pairs or small groups.
2. One student writes a letter in the air; the other guesses what letter it is.
3. Students take turns.

Variations & Tips

- You may want to have letters on slips of paper. A student draws a slip, but does not show anyone the letter drawn. The student writes the letter in the air and others guess. This could be done as a whole class or small group activity. This way, all letters will be practiced.
- Have one student say a letter, and the other write it in the air.
- Have students write whole words in the air.

Can You Spell That?

Proficiency Levels: Beginning

In this activity, teachers elicit information about students' lives while also asking them to spell out names and key words, providing practice with letters and spelling.

Steps

1. Ask students questions, such as the names of family members, where they live, and where they work.
2. For each name or place, ask "Can you spell that?" and have students spell the word while you write it on the board.

Variations & Tips
- Have a student take the place of the teacher, asking questions and saying "Can you spell that?", then writing names and places on the board.
- Practice spelling other word sets by asking a simple question, such as:
  - What do you like to eat?
  - What are you wearing?
  - What sports do you like?

Individual Journals

Proficiency Levels: High beginning+

In this activity, students write in journals to build writing fluency. Sharing journal entries with the teacher can foster a positive, nonthreatening relationship between student and teacher.

Steps
1. Students have notebooks or computer access in which they write journal entries.
2. Assign weekly or periodic journaling tasks which are either directed through a question or prompt or open to whatever the student wants to write about.
3. Collect the journals and write responses. Do not grade or correct the writing, but you may give tips and suggestions, or respond with interest and encouragement.
4. Note any language errors that could be addressed in future classes.

Variations & Tips
- Have students end their journal entries with a question for the teacher. This provides direction for your response and gives students an opportunity to have input into the dialogue.
- Give students a limited amount of time in class for writing their journal entries. Timed writing can increase fluency.
- When providing a prompt or topic for the journal writing, introduce the prompt in class first, providing time for students to orally brainstorm what they might write about.

Classroom Journals

Proficiency Levels: High beginning+

In this activity, students have access to a classroom journal in which they can write at any time. As all class members communicate with each other via the classroom journal, relationships are built, and the teacher is alerted to the thoughts and opinions of the students as a group.

Steps

1. Provides a notebook, which serves as the classroom journal.
2. Write the first entry, welcoming students to contribute to the journal and suggesting some topics of discussion.
3. Students access the journal whenever they have time, such as before or after class or when they have finished another task.
4. When writing, students should first read the last few journal entries, then write their own entry to continue the conversation.
5. Remind students periodically to read and write in the journal.
6. Occasionally read through the entries to know what is being discussed and possibly provide your own entry.

Variations & Tips

- Put a student in charge of the classroom journal. The student might be told to monitor the entries for appropriateness and to provide responses and prompts in the journal. This can be a weekly or monthly rotating role.
- Students can be encouraged to share photos, drawings, or other means of communicating their thoughts.
- When students share a home or preferred language, you can encourage them to write their entries in two or more languages.

Three-Stage Reading

Proficiency Levels: All

When engaging students in reading a text, the teacher leads students through pre-, during-, and postreading tasks.

Steps

1. Select a text at students' proficiency level. This normally means that no more than 5% of the words and structures are new for students.
2. Select and then facilitate tasks for all three reading phases, such as the following:

Prereading

- Students engage in a discussion to activate prior learning and experiences on the topic of the text. Students are prepared to draw connections between the reading and their own experiences and ideas.
- Students guess what they will discover in the reading.
- Students read the title and then write one thing that they hope to learn through the reading.

During Reading

- Students look for specific information as they are reading.
- Students look for specific grammatical forms or vocabulary as they are reading.
- Students underline phrases or ideas that stand out to them as they are reading.
- Students jot down questions they have as they read.

Postreading

- Students answer comprehension questions in pairs or groups.
- Students present questions about the reading to the whole class.
- Students write and share what they agreed with or disagreed with.
- Students retell the story or idea in their own words.
- Students write what might happen next.
- Students write or share how the reading might apply to their own life.

Variations & Tips

- Utilize translanguaging pedagogy as appropriate. For example, a prereading discussion might take place in the home language, with students then summarizing their discussion in English, or a final summary showing comprehension of the text might be written in the home language.

- Follow the three-stage approach for small sections of a text, not just for a text as a whole. For example, students could engage in the three stages for each point in an article.

- After students have learned several of the pre-, during-, and postreading strategies, let students take turns as "the teacher," selecting the strategies to be used.

Class Books

Proficiency Levels: High beginning+

Students create books telling about their lives or experiences, and classmates read each others' books.

Steps

1. Students write personal stories or narratives related to a topic of learning. For example, after learning words related to places and things in a house, a student might write a narrative as if he were showing someone around his house.

2. Check the writing and have students correct errors.

3. Students create booklets by folding together several pieces of paper.

4. Students copy their narratives into the booklet, adding photos or drawings. For example, an introduction to a student's home could be accompanied by photographs of the rooms in their house.

5. Students exchange and read books.

6. Provides postreading activities, such as questions about students' houses or playing a game showing photos of rooms as students say whose home it is.

Variations & Tips

- You can keep books and use them with future classes. If it is difficult to find reading materials at lower language proficiency levels, this is a good way to build up a library of easy-reading texts.

- Students can peer edit each others' stories or narratives before you check them.

- Students can create bilingual books, which could help to develop literacy in two languages.

- All students' narratives on a certain topic could be compiled into one book. In the given example, a class book could be created called "Our Homes." Copies could be made for all students, for them to practice reading at home.

Integrated Skills

In many ELT contexts, students want and need to learn all four skill areas—listening, speaking, reading, and writing—so it is often appropriate and beneficial to select activities that utilize all four skills.

The previous sections addressed oral skills and literacy skills separately. However, in reality, most of these activities could be altered in ways that integrate the four skills. For example, when students do a survey activity, they will not only be asking and answering questions, but they could also be writing answers on their survey forms. And when students do a sentence scramble, they might also talk with their group about the placement of the words and read their finished sentences aloud. Encouraging the use of all skills, even in ELT activities designed to practice just one or two skills, is usually valuable for MLEs; in the real world, we can't anticipate when and how language skills will overlap.

Some ELT activities lend themselves to a somewhat balanced practice of all skill areas, and these are the types of activities that are given in this section. Each activity here allows students to work on all skills. As with all activities in this book, be sure to choose materials that are at your MLEs' proficiency levels and that is of interest to them or related to your topic of study.

Tips

- ➤ Remember that even activities focusing on speaking and listening or reading and writing can usually be adapted to include all skills. For example, a reading activity could include pair or group discussion, and a pair speaking activity could include time to write a response before speaking.

- ➤ Activities that integrate multiple skills can allow students some choice in selecting skills for better comprehension or specific development. For example, a student might be given the resources to both hear and read language input, and can choose to focus more on one than the other.

- ➤ Integrated skills activities provide the opportunity to assess how well students can comprehend and use the same language in different skills. For example, a teacher might discover that students understand past verb forms when listening, but struggle to produce them in speaking and writing. This knowledge can help the teacher provide further focused practice activities using the past in speaking and writing.

Integrated Skills Activities

Read, Remember, Recite

Proficiency Levels: All

Instead of reading orally with eyes on the page, students read a sentence or phrase silently, but look up when they speak the sentence or phrase aloud. This fosters the notion of speaking to a real person while still providing the comfort of being given something to say.

Steps

1. Select a passage that is interesting for your students.

2. If sentences are long, break them into phrases.

3. Have each student read a sentence or phrase silently, then look up to say it to the class.

4. Have listeners write what their classmates say, or jot down key words.

Variations & Tips

- This can be a good way to read through dialogues because students must look at each other when they say their lines.
- Use this technique to help students practice for an oral presentation.

Song Key Words

Proficiency Levels: All

Students listen to songs, writing down key words as they hear them. Additional exercises on words or phrases in the song may follow.

Steps

1. Select a song and play it for your students. Have them write down one key word from each verse as they listen.
2. Repeat several times if necessary so students are able to hear and write at least one key word per verse.
3. After students have heard the song several times, invite them to sing along.

Variations & Tips

- Add vocabulary, reflection, or other types of exercises to the worksheet (see samples in Appendix B).
- Create a song cloze by finding or writing down the lyrics to the song and then deleting some key words on the worksheet.

Interviews

Proficiency Levels: All

Students are paired with one classmate to interview them and then write a summary paragraph.

Steps

1. Create a question and response chart (see the example in Appendix B) where students can log their questions and answers.

2. Have students write their interview questions. For students at early proficiency levels, three to five questions may be sufficient. Students at higher proficiency levels might have 10–15 questions or more, depending on the topic of the interview. The interview questions can be focused on a particular topic, such as places a person has lived, jobs they have done, or hobbies they enjoy.

3. Check the interview questions, correcting language as needed. Students can do some of this checking themselves, working in pairs or small groups, with the teacher visiting each group to confirm the accuracy of the sentences.

4. Place students in pairs. Have them take turns asking and answering their questions. Students should write in the answers on their response chart.

Variations & Tips

➤ After the interview, have students use a prepared paragraph template to write a paragraph about their interviewee. More advanced students can write a paragraph without a template.

➤ After the interview, have students tell about their partner to a small group or the whole class.

Dicto-Comp

Proficiency Levels: All

In this combination of dictation and composition (adapted from Wajnryb, 1988), students listen to a passage, then work in small groups to re-create the passage.

Steps

1. Select a short (three–four sentence) paragraph. The passage might also contain words or linguistic items that you want students to learn or practice.

2. Introduce the topic so that students will be prepared for the text. This could include asking questions, showing pictures, or introducing vocabulary words.

3. Read the paragraph to the students. Do not allow them to write anything down.

4. Read the paragraph again, allowing students to take notes. They should only write key words. (They must not write full sentences.) Repeat this step a few times, if necessary.

5. Ask students to rewrite the paragraph, based on their notes. Give them these guidelines:

   > Their writing should have the same ideas as the original.

   > Their writing should be grammatically correct.

   > Their writing does *not* need to be exactly like the paragraph you read.

6. In groups of three to four, students share their paragraphs and come up with a group version.

7. Students write their group versions on the board or on large paper, which can be put on the wall.

8. Read each paragraph as it is completed, underlining parts that may need work. Groups gather around their versions, correcting them and soliciting your help as needed. You may ask students to look at another group's work to help correct their own.

9. All groups read their paragraphs to the class.

Variations & Tips

- Have a student take on the role of teacher, selecting the passage and reading it to the class.
- Have students find similarities and differences between their passage and another group's, discussing the differences.

News Reports

Proficiency Levels: High beginning+

Students work in pairs or small groups to gather information then give a news report.

Steps

1. Place students in pairs or small groups and assign them a topic to report on. For example, they might give a weather forecast, tell about a sports event, or provide information about a store that is opening soon.
2. Students do research on their topic. You may give them materials to read or you can ask them to do research.
3. Students write out their report on the topic.
4. Check what students have written.
5. In pairs or small groups, students practice "reporting" on their topic: They read aloud what they have written multiple times. Classmates listen and provide feedback on language use and/or content.
6. Create something that looks like a "News Station" at the front of the classroom.
7. The pairs or groups take turns giving their reports.

Variations & Tips

- Reports might be given "live," with students in the "audience" asking the speaker questions, as if they are reporters.
- Reports can be video-recorded. Students can watch their reports and make a list of pronunciation or language items that they want to work on.
- Students listening to the reports might write headlines for them.

Relay Races

Proficiency Levels: Beginning

Competing teams form relay lines. They run to the front and must match several words on cards with real items or pictures, saying the words as they match them.

Steps

1. Place students in two teams. Teams line up.
2. Provide three to four words on cards, and the corresponding real items or pictures, at the front of each team. The items are not matched. For example, you might provide the words *hat, belt, glove,* and *sunglasses,* and all of these real items.
3. When the relay starts, one person from each team runs up and matches each word with its item or picture, saying the words aloud.
4. Check items. If they are matched correctly, the student rescrambles the words and items or pictures, and runs back to the team, and the next person in line runs up. When each team member has done the matching successfully, the team is done.
5. The team that finishes first wins.
6. To extend into listening, say the word shown on each picture and have the student point to the right picture.
7. To extend into writing, remove the words on cards. Instead, provide a white board on which the student will write the names of the items in the pictures.

Variations & Tips

- Students could have to say a short sentence or phrase, not just the word. For example, the student might have to say "This is a belt" or "These are sunglasses."
- Students might have to do something with the objects and say what they are doing. For example, they might have to put on the belt, while saying "I'm putting on the belt," and then take off the belt while saying "I'm taking off the belt."
- Students might pass objects to each other, instead of running to the front. For example, they might pass the gloves and the card with the word *gloves,* while saying "These are gloves." When all objects are passed through the whole line, the team is finished.

Scavenger Hunt

Proficiency Levels: Beginning

Pairs or teams compete to find a list of items that have been previously hidden, or which are naturally present in or outside of the classroom.

Steps

1. Select the items the students will look for.
2. Place students in pairs or teams and give each a list of what they should look for.
3. Teams look for the items, checking them off on their list when they find them, and possibly also collecting them. For example, if you've hidden items or pictures around the room to practice certain vocabulary, students will just check off the items on their list as they find them. But if you've asked them to collect the items, they would bring them to you when they have found them all. Examples:
    - Hide food items around the room. Students check off each food item on their list when they see it; they do not remove it.
    - Hide pictures of animals around the room. Students check off each animal on their list when they see it; they do not remove the picture.
    - Don't hide anything, but put items on the list that students can find in the classroom: pencil, pen, ruler, chalk, eraser, and so on.
    - Don't hide anything, but put items on the list that students can find outside the classroom: leaf, twig, stone, dirt, and so on.
4. As teams complete the activity, have them report to you. Ask them where each item is. They need to respond with sentences such as these:
    - "We found the apple. It is in the corner behind the plant."
    - "We found the picture of the elephant. It was under your desk."
    - "We didn't find the picture of the monkey."
    - "We found a leaf."
    - "We couldn't find a stone."
5. To extend into writing, have students write out the location of each item.

Variations & Tips

- "Scavenger Photos" is a variation in which students try to take photos of items on the list. This can be used for students with a little higher proficiency. For example, an outdoor scavenger list might include items such as: a broken fence, a cloud the shape of something, a wall painted blue, a street sign. Emotion words can also be practiced as students take pictures of people role-playing emotions, such as being angry, bored, happy, or interested. At a higher level, students could practice adjectives, such as *ecstatic, disinterested, jubilant, frustrated*.

- Comparatives and superlatives can be practiced by having students collect items that will then be compared among teams. For example, the scavenger list might request: the longest branch, the prettiest flower, the most colorful bug, and so on. Students compare and vote on the collected items, and teams with the winning item in any category earns points.

Video TPR

Proficiency Levels: Intermediate

Pairs or teams create videos fulfilling a written list of commands.

Steps

1. Provide, both orally and in writing, a list of commands that students can role-play. These might be for a process, such as doing laundry, or they might be successive related commands, such as going through a stretching routine.
2. Students take turns acting out the commands and video-recording.
3. Teams show the class their video-recording, narrating what they are doing as they show the recording. Classmates listen and write down the commands they see enacted in the video.

Variations & Tips

- Students might write their own list of commands, showing them to you before they begin recording.

> Have students brainstorm processes that they want to know how to talk about in English. For example, they might want to know how to explain how a food item from their culture is prepared. Have students work in groups to watch each other simulate each step, then work together to formulate commands that describe the steps. Groups could then exchange commands, having other groups follow their steps, with real or simulated actions.

Perspectives

Proficiency Levels: Intermediate/Advanced

In this activity, students are placed in small groups and asked to solve a problem, with each person bringing in a different perspective on the problem.

Steps

1. Identify a problem or issue that students are interesting in discussing. For example, you might present the problem, "How much homework should students have?"

2. Write short paragraphs identifying different perspectives on the issue. For example, in the given example issue, the perspectives might be those of a student, teacher, parent, and principal. Each person in the group receives a different perspective.

3. Taking on the role representing their perspective, students must discuss the issue, and come up with a solution or resolution.

4. Groups present their solutions to the class, showing how all perspectives were taken into account.

5. Students write out their solution in a short paragraph.

Variations & Tips

> Groups can be given the same problem to solve, or different problems. If groups are given different problems, these might feed into a larger problem-based learning activity. For example, if students are asked to help solve the problem of homelessness in their city, groups might be given problems on different topics: shelters, employment services, mental health facilities, health, and safety.

➤ A shorter version of this activity can be done in pairs, with two different perspectives on an issue. For example, students might "debate" the perspectives of using the home language during English class or not using it, and might come up with a balanced perspective to share with the class.

NO!

Proficiency Levels: Intermediate

Students write rebuttals using negatives, then must quickly use these negative statements in a fast-paced circle game.

Steps

1. Introduce a scenario for producing sentences. These can be real or humorous, such as:

    a. Why did the chicken cross the road?

    b. Who is going to win the World Cup?

    c. What is the best dessert?

2. Write a one-sentence response on the board, then have students write their own responses. For example:

    a. The chicken crossed the road to visit her grandmother.

    b. Cameroon is going to win the World Cup.

    c. Passionfruit mousse is the best dessert.

3. Put the "rebuttal" sentence on the board. For example:

    a. No! The chicken didn't cross the road to visit her grandmother. She crossed the road to see a movie!

    b. No! Cameroon is not going to win the World Cup. Brazil is going to win the World Cup!

    c. No! Passionfruit mousse is not the best dessert. Chocolate cake is the best dessert!

4. Students sit in the circle. Provide a soft ball or toy for tossing. Begin by saying your statement. Then, throw the ball to a student. The student must respond with a rebuttal statement.

5. The student then throws the ball to another student, who must contradict the last student's statement and provide their own.

6. Play continues as the ball is thrown to different students.

Variations & Tips

- You can be intentional in having students practice different verb tenses, as illustrated in the steps. Modals can also be practiced through scenarios such as these:
  - What can you do with a paper clip? (Sample responses: You can pick a lock. No! You can't pick a lock. You can use it as a bookmark.)
  - What would the Loch Ness Monster eat for lunch? (Sample responses: He would eat sandwiches. No! He wouldn't eat sandwiches. He would eat spaghetti.)

- This activity can help to practice complex sentences with multiple clauses. For example:
  - Why did the chicken cross the road? She crossed the road because she wanted to visit her grandmother.
  - No! She didn't cross the road because she wanted to visit her grandmother. She crossed the road because she wanted to see a movie.

Expert Groups

Proficiency Levels: All

Each student in a group becomes an "expert" on an aspect of a topic, then shares their expertise with their group.

Steps

1. Identify an issue or topic. For example, the topic might be "nutrition."
2. Identify a final group outcome. For example: "Create a balanced 1-day meal plan."
3. Identify several areas of expertise. In this example, there could be four areas of expertise: carbohydrates, proteins, fats, and vitamins and minerals.
4. Place students in groups with the number of students matching the number of areas of expertise. In this example, there would be four students per group.
5. Give students, in writing and orally, the expert topics. Have students identify which group members will take which topics.
6. Have students regroup into expert groups. In this example, there would be groups for: carbohydrates, proteins, fats, and vitamins and minerals. Provide information in writing about that topic for each group. Have students read through it together and write out questions they have.
7. Go around to each expert group and answer their questions.
8. Have students return to their original groups, where each student shares their expertise.
9. Have students complete the assigned task, utilizing each person's expertise. In this example, students would be applying their learning about carbohydrates, proteins, fats, and vitamins and minerals to create a one-day meal plan.
10. To further extend learning, groups could compare their meal plan with another group's meal plan, writing about the similarities and differences.

Variations & Tips

- In contexts where students share a home language, it might be appropriate to provide the "expertise" in the home language. After the content is understood, students can work in their expert groups to frame the content in English, to share with their original group.

- Instead of a final group product, such as a menu, you can give students a worksheet. Give each "expert" information to complete a part of the worksheet, then have them share that expertise with their group.

- This activity is a good opportunity to introduce new content in a way that is student centered, rather than teacher centered.

Chapter Summary

This chapter has provided additional information on helping students develop listening, speaking, reading, and writing skills. It also provided a starting point for understanding and implementing many different activities to help students use and develop language. This is just a sampling of many language acquisition activities that can be found in English learning materials and online. As you teach, you will find many ways to adapt these and other activities for specific groups of learners.

CHAPTER 7

Charting a Course for ELT Development

This book began by providing an introduction to language and to language acquisition. It then looked at the many differences in both English language teaching (ELT) contexts and in the learners themselves. Finally, it introduced language teaching processes, techniques, and methods, from initial planning through to assessment.

Perhaps this information has given you a basic understanding of the ELT profession, but you may also now realize that there is much more to learn! This chapter provides information about types and means of preparation in the field of ELT and highlights steps you can take to further your learning and skills.

Levels of Training

Anyone searching the internet for training in ELT can quickly become overwhelmed and confused by the many options and marketing ploys. This section highlights levels of training, and jobs and activities appropriate for each level. Then, it provides program features, and types and examples of training programs.

Training in teaching the English language ranges from weekend seminars to advanced degrees. Each level functions in a different way to equip those who work with multilingual learners of English (MLEs). The following list presents training options from the least to the most training.

Short Seminars, Workshops, and Conferences

Language schools (schools that provide language instruction, not regular schooling), universities, or individual speakers sometimes provide seminars and workshops on ELT. These could be a just a few hours, a weekend, or a few days in length. These types of opportunities can help those who work with MLEs grow in their knowledge and skill, perhaps in specific areas, such as "activities to build oral skills" or "correcting student writing." However, they should not be viewed as sufficient training for those who are teaching the English langauge on a regular basis or who are involved in activities such as program design, curricular decisions, and placement testing.

Certificate

Perhaps the most well-known credential for teaching English, worldwide, is the certificate. Unfortunately, there has been little oversight as to what content an ELT certificate needs to provide. Indeed, even its name varies widely:

- TESOL certificate (teaching English to speakers of other languages)
- TEFL certificate (teaching English as a foreign language)
- TESL certificate (teaching English as a second language)
- ELT certificate (English language teaching)

TESOL International Association (2015) has developed standards for a TESOL certificate (*Standards for Short-Term TEFL/TESL Certificate Programs: With Program Assessment*). The publication includes extensive standards for organization and program management, curriculum and instructors, and candidates. In short, following are some hallmarks of a certificate that meets the standards:

Hallmarks of a Certificate Program for Teaching English

- At least 100 hours of study
- Instruction and applied learning, at an introductory level, in the areas of
  - Second Language Acquisition
  - Linguistics
  - English Grammar
  - Culture
  - Lesson Planning
  - Lesson Delivery
  - Assessment

➤ A practicum experience of at least 20 hours, which includes at least 10 hours of teaching.

Bachelor's Degree

In many countries, the most common preparation for becoming an English language teacher is by getting a bachelor's degree at a university. This degree might have different names in different countries, such as a bachelor's in language teaching, ELT, TEFL, TESL, or TESOL. This type of training may include developing proficiency in English and then taking courses such as those on the hallmarks list, but with more extensive study. A person with this type of training from a reputable and well-designed program is fully prepared as a teacher of English.

Master's or Doctoral Degree

Those who envision a career in ELT often go on to get a master's degree in TESOL, ELT, second language acquisition, linguistics, or other similar content. Because some graduate programs in this field accept students with undergraduate degrees in many different fields, the level of instruction in ELT at the graduate level varies a great deal. Some graduate programs may have similar levels of instruction to bachelor-level programs, while others offer higher levels of specialization in specific areas of ELT without any duplication of undergraduate learning. Doctoral programs nearly always provide the opportunity for specialization in a specific area of ELT.

Advanced degrees in the teaching of language are usually needed for university-level teaching positions, and for positions involving research, publishing, designing curricula, and creating and leading programs.

Other Higher Education Training

In addition to coursework and degrees in ELT, many universities offer other programs with ELT specializations within them, such as in education, cross-cultural or international studies, and business. Some universities offer TESOL training at the certificate level. Some also provide other levels of instruction, such as minors, concentrations, or tracks within bachelor's and master's degree programs.

Some universities have ELT preparation programs that operate fairly independently from the university itself. An example of this type of program is CELTA (Certificate in English Language Teaching to Adults; www.teachinghouse.com/courses/the-celta-course) and

DELTA (Diploma in English Language Teaching to Adults; www.cambridgeenglish.org/teaching-english/teaching-qualifications/delta), both under the umbrella of Cambridge University and the PCELT (Professional Certificate in English Language Teaching), created by SIT World Learning and offered by Amideast.

Other higher education institutions have programs within their regular departments. For example, training to become an English language teacher might be found in the Education Department or the English Department. In many countries, there are state/province, federal, and private higher education universities, each with its own type of English language program. The perceived quality and rigor of private and public universities, and the costs associated with each, vary within each country.

Types of Training Programs

Training programs for teaching English that are not provided within higher education systems are typically provided by independent associations, schools, or companies that are solely focused on the training of English language teachers. Such programs usually offer certificate-level training in ELT and may also offer short seminars and workshops. An example of such a program is TESOL International Association's Core Certificate Program (see www.tesol.org/tccp). It provides both instructed and self-paced online options.

Programs that are not offered through higher education institutions vary a great deal in quality and legitimacy. Those offered by professional associations gain credibility from the association. Well-known associations and schools can be good sources of certificate-level training and may be less expensive than university programs. Some independent companies offer strong programs for training certificates, and they perhaps provide courses at a cheaper rate than better known institutions. There are also, however, independent companies seeking to make money rather than provide quality instruction. Using the list of program hallmarks earlier in this chapter can ensure that you find an effective training program.

Features of Training Programs

As you consider which program and program type will meet your ELT needs, it's important to consider the features of different programs. Some questions to ask include the following:

Online or On-site

- Is the program online or on-site?
- How much of the instruction is online versus onsite?

- Is it a hybrid program?
- Is the online instruction synchronous (participants are virtually present at the same time) or asynchronous (participants are not present at the same time, but interact through tools, such as discussion boards).
- What learning management system is used?

Scheduled or Self-Paced

- Do I go through the program at my own pace, or are there deadlines and due dates for work and classroom experiences?
- If self-paced, how much time do I have to finish the course?
- If scheduled, how long is the program? How frequent are classroom experiences? How often will I be turning in assignments?

Instructed or Self-Taught

- Will I interact with a teacher and/or a cohort of peers, or will I be going through course content on my own?
- Will a teacher provide feedback on my work, or will computerized grading be used?

These are just some of the characteristics of different programs. There are many more components that might bear investigation, such as the cost of the program and materials, the use of physical books or online resources, and the level of training and experience of the instructors or professors.

Professional Associations

Joining a professional association can provide many opportunities for ongoing development in ELT. An internet search of professional organizations in your area can let you know what organizations are available locally, in your country or region. Here are two well-known international associations:

- **International Association of Teachers of English as a Foreign Language** (IATEFL; www.iatefl.org): IATEFL has teaching associates around the world.
- **TESOL International Association** (www.tesol.org): TESOL International Association also has affiliate organizations around the world.

Professional associations can help you connect to other professionals locally and internationally. Many associations have email groups, professional learning networks, and other resources for discussing topics of interest in the field. Many provide free resources on a broad range of ELT topics on their websites or through links to other sites. Finally, many also host conferences and seminars to help you grow as an ELT professional.

Continuing Your Learning

If you picked up this book and read through it to the end, it's probably because you are interested in learning more about the ELT field. Perhaps you have not taught English at all, but are curious about it and considering it as a vocation. Perhaps you have done some English teaching as a volunteer and are realizing that there is a lot to learn about how to do it well. Perhaps you have several MLEs in your math class. Perhaps you've had some training in teaching English, but would like to learn more or go deeper into the content.

If you are ready to take the next step in your journey, first consider the role you think you might want to have in the field of ELT. Do you just want to be prepared to help MLEs informally by providing conversation practice or tutoring? If so, you might find webinars, conferences, and additional books that can equip you in specific ways. TESOL Press has published a series of books and other resources entitled "The 6 Principles for Exemplary Teaching of English Learners®." The series includes versions for many different contexts, including teaching children in English-medium schooling, teaching children in EFL settings, teaching adults in workplace programs, and others. If you would like to read more about ELT, The 6 Principles text for your context would be a good next step. (Read more about The 6 Principles on the companion website, www.tesol.org/ELTBasics.)

Are you considering a career in ELT, teaching in an educational institution? If so, you will probably want to pursue at least a certificate, if not a full degree program.

When you are ready, you can further your learning by finding seminars that might be offered near you, and by joining an ELT professional association, whether your local chapter or an international organization. There are also many videos and webinars offered free, online. Appendix C has some resources on teaching English as an additional language to get you started. If you do decide to pursue further formal training, you may want to start with a short certificate. If you continue on, you might want to add a degree in ELT. No matter what your ELT future holds, you have taken the first step by reading this book.

Chapter Summary

Teaching English effectively requires training. Perhaps reading this book is your first venture into the world of English teaching, and now you are ready to pursue training. The following can help direct your search:

- Training in ELT ranges from short seminars to university degree programs.
- Different levels of training are needed for different ELT contexts and purposes. A short seminar may be sufficient to help you become an effective conversation partner for an English learner, but a degree in ELT is needed to create English learning programs and design curricula.
- One of the most common levels of training is the TESOL/TEFL/TESL Certificate. These are abundant, but must be vetted well for quality.
- The "Hallmarks" list can help you to determine the quality of a training program.
- Training programs vary as to how they are delivered, with many options for fully online, hybrid, or fully in-person programs.

Conclusion

The field of ELT is diverse. The level and type of training that one needs in different teaching situations can be different from country to country, and even within different regions of the same country. However, it's nearly always the case that MLEs are best served by having teachers who have some training in teaching English as an additional language. You have begun that training journey by reading this book, and hopefully now will continue as you begin to discover the vast resources that are available in the field of ELT.

Glossary

These terms are defined as they relate to language teaching and learning.

Affective filter: Framing of stressors as a "filter" that prevents language input when raised.

Assessment: Determining what language has been learned or acquired.

Automaticity: Ability to understand or produce language quickly and easily, without stopping to think about it.

Code-switching: Switching between languages when speaking or writing (often confused with *translanguaging*).

Communicative language teaching: Classroom instruction that focuses on using language rather than learning about language.

Comprehensible input: Language heard or read that is understood because it is only slightly above the learner's level, or because visuals are used to aid comprehension.

Content and language integrated learning: Learning academic content in a language that is being acquired; instruction purposefully both teaches content and helps students acquire language.

Content-based instruction: Language instruction in which lessons are centered around content (e.g., cooking, web design, business management) that is motivating for learners.

Dialect: Variations within a language, typically due to geographical separation.

Fluency: Using language in speaking and writing without unnatural pauses that disrupt communication; comprehending language in listening and reading without pauses which disrupt comprehension.

Form: One aspect of language—its structure.

Formative assessment: Observations of student language use within classroom instruction; used to tailor future instruction to student needs.

Input: Language that students hear and/or read; used when talking about students receiving language.

Interaction: Students using the target language to communicate with each other and with the teacher in class.

L1/L2: First language/second language.

Language community: A group of people who use language in the same way.

Language domains: The language skills of reading, writing, speaking, and listening.

Language focus: Teaching and learning that focuses on discrete language items, such as grammar and pronunciation.

Language proficiency level: The amount of language a person knows and can use for communication.

Lesson objectives: The aims of a lesson; how students will use language during the lesson, or what they will be able to do using language as a result of the lesson.

Meaning: One aspect of language—the ideas that the language communicates.

Natural sequence: The order in which learners acquire components of a new language.

Output: Language that students speak or write; used when talking about students producing language.

Phonology: The system of sounds within a language.

Placement testing: Evaluating a person's language knowledge and skills for the purpose of placing them in appropriate classes or levels.

Practicality: An aspect of assessment that considers feasibility and logistics in using the assessment.

Productive skills: Speaking and writing skills; how a person produces language.

Receptive skills: Listening and reading skills; how a person receives language.

Reliability: A quality of assessment—an assessment produces the same results every time it is given.

Rubric: A tool providing the criteria on which the assessment of student language use and/or an assignment is based.

Scaffold: A support in learning; something that helps a learner acquire new knowledge or skill.

Second language acquisition: The field of study concerning how people learn new languages; the process of learning a new language.

Stress: Difficult circumstances that may cause negative emotions and make it challenging for a learner to acquire language.

Structures: Grammatical forms of language.

Summative assessment: Determining the language learned or acquired at the end of a period of instruction (the summation of learning).

Target language: The language that is being learned or acquired.

Task-based language teaching: Classroom learning in which students focus on completing a task, acquiring new language as it is needed in order to complete the task.

Translanguaging: When students utilize their full linguistic repertoire, including linguistic features of multiple languages, to maximize communication (often confused with *code-switching*).

Use: One aspect of language—how concepts and ideas are communicated.

Validity: A quality of assessment—that an assessment measures what it claims to measure.

Washback: The effect of assessment on instruction; the ways in which the use of a particular type of assessment drives teachers to select content for classroom instruction.

Zone of proximal development: Theory by Vygotsky (1978); the zone is the distance between what a learner can do on their own and what they can do only with support.

References

Asher, J. (1969). The total physical response approach to second language learning. *The Modern Language Journal, 53*(1), 3–17. https://doi.org/10.2307/322091

Bailey, F., & Pransky, K. (2013). *Implications and applications of the latest brain research for English language learners and teachers* [Webinar]. TESOL International Association. https://www.tesol.org/events-landing-page/2013/01/30/implications-and-applications-of-the-latest-brain-research-for-english-language-learners-and-teachers

Brown, H. D., & Lee, H. (2015). *Teaching by principles: An interactive approach to language pedagogy* (4th ed.). Pearson.

Chomsky, N. (1959). Review of "Verbal Behavior" by B.F. Skinner. *Language, 35,* 26–58.

Cummins, J. (2000). *Language, power, and pedagogy: Bilingual children in the crossfire (bilingual education & bilingualism, 23)*. Multilingual Matters.

Krashen, S. (1977). Some issues relating to the monitor model. In H. D. Brown, C. A. Yorio, & R. H. Crymes (Eds.), *On TESOL '77* (pp. 144–158). Teachers of English to Speakers of Other Languages.

Krashen, S. (1981). *Second language acquisition and second language learning*. Pergamon.

Krashen, S., & Terrell, T. (1983). *The natural approach: Language acquisition in the classroom*. Alemany Press.

Kuhl, P. K. (2010). Brain mechanisms in early language acquisition. *Neuron, 67*(5), 713–727. https://doi.org/10.1016/j.neuron.2010.08.038

Lenneberg, E. H. (1967). *Biological foundations of language*. Wiley.

Lightbown, P. M., & Spada, N. (2013). *How languages are learned*. Oxford University Press.

Long, M. H. (1981). Input, interaction, and second-language acquisition. *Annals of the New York academy of sciences, 379*(1), 259–278. https://doi.org/10.1111/j.1749-6632.1981.tb42014.x

McHugh, M., Gelatt, J., & Fix, M. (2007). *Adult English language instruction in the United States: Determining need and investing wisely*. Migration Policy Institute. https://www.migrationpolicy.org/pubs/NCIIP_English_Instruction073107.pdf

Nation, I. S. P., & Macalister, J. (2020). *Teaching ESL/EFL reading and writing* (2nd ed.). Routledge.

Nation, I. S. P., & Newton, J. M. (2020). *Teaching ESL/EFL listening and speaking* (2nd ed.). Routledge.

Piaget, J. (1951). *Play, dreams and imitation in childhood* (Gattegno & F. M. Hodgson, Trans.). Heinneman. (Original work published 1946)

Ray, B. (1990). *Look, I can talk!* Sky Oaks.

Richards, J. C., & Rodgers, T. S. (2001). *Approaches and methods in language teaching* (2nd ed.). Cambridge University Press.

Skinner, B. F. (1957). *Verbal behavior*. Appleton-Century-Crofts.

Snow, C., & Hoefnagel-Hohle, M. (1982). The critical period for language acquisition: Evidence from second language learning. In S. Krashen, R. Scarcell, & M. Long (Eds.), *Issues in second language research* (pp. 93–113). Newbury House.

Snow, D. (2007). *From language learner to language teacher: An introduction to teaching English as a foreign language*. Teachers of English to Speakers of Other Languages.

Swain, M. (1985). Communicative competence: Some roles of comprehensible input and comprehensible output in its development. In S. Gass & C. Madden (Eds.), *Input in second language acquisition* (pp. 235–253). Newbury House.

TESOL International Association. (2015). *Standards for short-term TEFL/TESL certificate programs: With program assessment*. TESOL Press.

Vygotsky, L. S. (1978). *Mind in society*. Harvard University Press.

Wajnryb, R. (1988). The dictogloss method of language teaching: A text-based, communicative approach to grammar. *English Teaching Forum, 26*(3), 35–38.

APPENDIX A

Acronyms in TESOL

Acronym	Meaning	Usage
ACTFL	Formerly "American Council of Teachers of Foreign Languages" (Now ACTFL)	Resource for standards, proficiency levels and curriculum guides for the teaching of world languages
CEA	Commission on English Language Program Accreditation	An accreditor of programs that teach English as an additional language
EAL	English as an additional language	Replacing "ESL" in some contexts
EAP	English for academic purposes	Often used for secondary and postsecondary study that is specifically oriented toward preparation for university studies in English
EFL	English as a foreign language	English learning in countries which do not have English as a national or dominant language; English is typically learned as a foreign language subject in school
EIL	English as an international language	Sometimes used to refer to English taught and used for global communication
ELL or EL	English language learner or English learner	Used to refer to students of English, especially in ESL contexts
ELT	English language teaching	Can be used to refer to the field of study, as in "a conference on ELT"
ENL	English as a new language	Replacing "ESL" in some places, in recognition that for many students English is not a second, but a third or fourth language

Acronym	Meaning	Usage
ESL	English as a second language	English learning in countries which have English as a national or dominant language; English is typically learned by children in school or by adults in programs for immigrants
ESOL	English to speakers of other languages	A term that can be used instead of both "ESL" and "EFL"; thus, it is increasingly used when speaking of all English learning contexts
IELTS	International English Language Testing System	A test to determine English proficiency
MLE	Multilingual learner of English	An asset-based term used to refer to learners of English as an additional language
MLL	Multilingual language learner	Sometimes used in English-medium schools to refer students who are learning English
SLA	Second language acquisition	The study of how people learn new languages
TEFL	Teaching English as a foreign language	Can be used to refer to the field of study, as in "Certificate in TEFL"
TESL	Teaching English as a second language	Can be used to refer to the field of study, as in "Certificate in TESL"
TESOL*	Teaching English to speakers of other languages	Used to refer to the field of study, as in "Master's degree in TESOL"
TOEFL	Test of English as a Foreign Language	An English test that is usually taken by foreign students to gain entrance into American universities
WIDA	Formerly "World-Class Instructional Design and Assessment" (Now WIDA)	A set of standards and testing to determine English proficiency of students in K–12 settings

*Note that *TESOL International Association* is an international professional organization of English teachers, based in the United States. It is sometimes referred to simply as "TESOL."

APPENDIX B

Sample Worksheets

Worksheet 1. Song Key Words

LEAN ON ME

Key Words

In each verse of the song,[1] write down one key word that you hear. For example, in the first phrase, "Lean on me, when you're not strong" you might write "lean" and "strong."

Idioms

Match the phrases with the definitions:

to continue	lean on
count on / rely on	call on
ask for help	carry on

Use the idioms to fill in the blanks below.

1. Can I _____ you if I need help?
2. Don't _____ on that fence. It's broken.
3. My job is difficult, but I will _____.

---

1. Bill Withers. (1972). Lean on me [song]. On *Still Bill*. Sussex.

Questions

1. When do you "lean on" others? _____

2. Can others "lean on" you? How and when? _____

Create Motions

With a partner, create motions to the song. Act out "leaning" on a friend, being "strong," etc.

Sing the Song!

Find the song online, and sing along!

Worksheet 2. Surveys

Q: Do you like _____?
A: Yes, I like _____.
No, I don't like _____.

Name	bananas	apples	papaya	pineapple
Mario	✓	✓	✗	✓

Worksheet 3. Interviews

Write About Your Friend!

Ask your friend:

Information You Need	Question to Ask	Answer
Name		
Country		
Age		
Birthday		
Sisters		
Brothers		
Hobbies		

My friend is _____. _____ comes from _____. _____ is _____ years old. _____ birthday is on _____. _____ has _____ sisters and _____ brothers. _____ likes to _____. I like my new _____!

Worksheet 4. Find Someone Who

How do your classmates cope with stress? Find someone who…

1. writes in a journal   Name: _____

   Question prompt: **Do you…..?**

2. talks to a friend   Name: _____

3. talks to a family member   Name: _____

4. eats ice cream   Name: _____

5. goes shopping Name: _____

6. goes running Name: _____

7. reads a book Name: _____

8. other: _____ Name: _____

Write in your answers to the questions, then talk with a partner about your responses:

Do any of your classmates cope with stress in the same way that you do?
_____

Would you like to change how you cope with stress?
_____

Does your partner have any advice for coping with stress?
_____

APPENDIX C

Resources

Resources on teaching English as an additional language are plentiful on the internet. Here are some well-known websites to get you started.

ACTFL
www.actfl.org
ACTFL provides descriptions of proficiency levels and video clips of real learners demonstrating those levels. This organization also provides information on teaching resources, assessment of language skills, and information on professionalization as a language teacher. ACTFL conducts conferences and workshops for language teachers, and provides ways and means to advocate for language instruction.

Center for Applied Linguistics (CAL)
www.cal.org
The CAL website includes many briefs and digests on hundreds of topics related to language learning and teaching. The organization also provides conferences and workshops for English language teachers.

Colorín Colorado
www.colorincolorado.org
Colorín Colorado is a website that has practical resources for teachers and families on topics related to the education of English language learners in primary and secondary education. It has resources for those who do not have training in English language teaching (ELT) and also provides information that is helpful for professionals in the field. It has many resources to use with families and within schools.

Dave's ESL Café
www.eslcafe.com

Dave Sperling is the creator of this well-known website on all things ELT-related. From jobs in ELT around the globe to training options to lesson plans, this website provides rich resources and information for those in the field of ELT.

TESOL International Association (TESOL)
www.tesol.org

TESOL International Association provides many types of resources for those in ELT around the globe. The website provides papers outlining position statements on many topics, many different kinds of training courses, information about conferences, and a robust job board. TESOL's publishing arm, TESOL Press, includes hundreds of titles on ELT. TESOL International Association has affiliates around the world, and links to these organizations can be found on the website.

www.ingramcontent.com/pod-product-compliance
Ingram Content Group UK Ltd.
Pitfield, Milton Keynes, MK11 3LW, UK
UKHW022211230426
12048UKWH00016BA/783